SOPRINTENDENZA ARCHEOL

DISCOVERING
POMPEII

ITINERARIES FOR VISITORS
ON THE OCCASION OF THE 250TH ANNIVERSARY
OF THE BEGINNING OF THE EXCAVATIONS

edited by
Antonio d'Ambrosio

ELECTA

**250th anniversary of the beginning
of the excavations at Pompeii
1748-1998**

*Cover: F. Mazois,
View of the Large Theater
(Mazois, IV, pl. XXX)*

© 1998 Ministero per i Beni Culturali e Ambientali
Soprintendenza Archeologica di Pompei
Published by Electa, Milano
Elemond Editori Associati

It is not an easy task to look back a quarter of a millennium. How can the observer free his gaze from the bias of the present? How can one be sure that one's judgement is historically correct and not influenced by the consequences that those remote events had, independently of the intentions of the first excavators?
Methodological coherence is a prerequisite for every investigation based on a methodology. But method teaches us that data are only a part of the research. Alongside the patient and meticulous collecting of data, there should be an effort to understand the bias resulting from the fact that the student of antiquity lives in the present and, if it were not so, he would not be a man, but a machine. And they were men too, those military engineers, those diggers, those forced laborers who, unaware of the significance of their action, set out on an enterprise that was to last 250 years. As they laid the foundation for an investigation which remains unparalleled in the story of archaeological studies, they worked under the bias of their own present. The information they left us bears this clearly out, beginning from their incertitude as to the ancient name (Pompeii?

Stabiae?) of what they were bringing to light. Thus, in recalling today those ancient beginnings, besides collecting the data they produced, we also look back to them as a useful source of reflection upon our present. A present in which the Archaeological Superintendency of Pompeii has entered a new phase of autonomous self-management allowing it to intensify its activities for the preservation, exploration and development of the site. This gives special significance to the 250th anniversary of the beginning of the excavations at Pompeii. A comparison between these two analogous situations and, of course, an examination of the results obtained by the ancient excavators can help us to deal with the difficulties of this new situation.
We are not counting on somebody to remember us 250 years from now. We are merely aware that we belong to a lineage of archaeologists who have assumed specific and clear-cut responsibilities, and thanks to whom Pompeii is known all over the world.

Pietro Giovanni Guzzo
Archaeological Superintendent of Pompeii

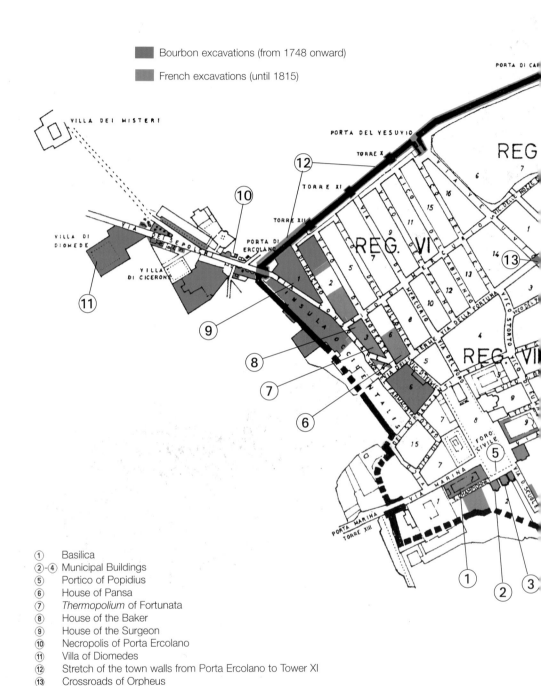

Bourbon excavations (from 1748 onward)

French excavations (until 1815)

VILLA DEI MISTERI

VILLA DI DIOMEDE

VILLA DI CICERONE

PORTA DI CA...

PORTA DEL VESUVIO

TORRE X

TORRE XI

TORRE XII

PORTA DI ERCOLANO

REG...

REG. VI

REG. VI...

VIA DEI SEPOLCRI

INSULA OCCIDENTALIS

VIA CONSOLARE

VICO DI MERCURIO

VICO DELLA FULLONICA

VICO DEL LABIRINTO

VICO DEL FAUNO

VICO STORTO

VIA DELLA FORTUNA

TERME DEL FORO

VIA DEL FORO

FORO CIVILE

VIA MARINA

VIA D...

PORTA MARINA
TORRE XIII

① Basilica
②-④ Municipal Buildings
⑤ Portico of Popidius
⑥ House of Pansa
⑦ *Thermopolium* of Fortunata
⑧ House of the Baker
⑨ House of the Surgeon
⑩ Necropolis of Porta Ercolano
⑪ Villa of Diomedes
⑫ Stretch of the town walls from Porta Ercolano to Tower XI
⑬ Crossroads of Orpheus
⑭ Temple of Isis
⑮ Samnite Gymnasium
⑯ Triangular Forum
⑰ *Porticus post scaenam*
⑱ Large Theater
⑲ *Odeion*
⑳ Temple of Jupiter Meilichios
㉑ Amphitheater

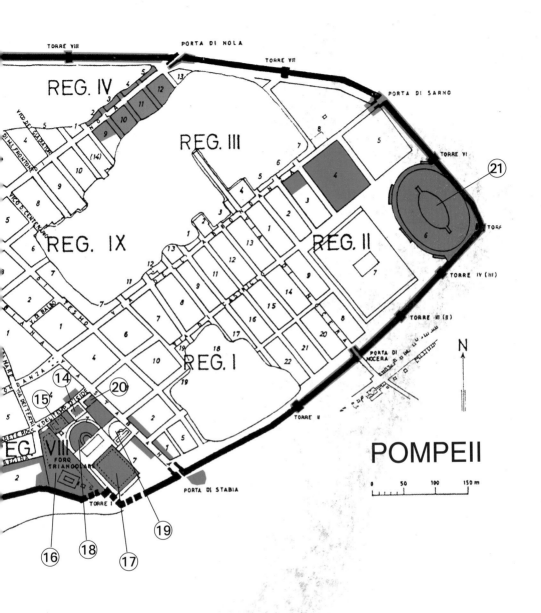

TORRE VIII   PORTA DI NOLA   TORRE VII   PORTA DI SARNO

REG. IV

REG. III

REG. IX

REG. II

REG. I

TORRE VI

TORRE

TORRE IV (III)

TORRE III (II)

PORTA DI NOCERA

TORRE II

PORTA DI STABIA

TORRE I

EG. VIII
FORO
TRIANGOLARE

POMPEII

N

0   50   100   150 m

EXCAVATIONS FROM 1748 TO 1815

According to a rather worn-out cliché based on hindsight, the early excavations undertaken in the Vesuvian area at the behest of the Bourbons was the antithesis of model archaeological research.

Entire buildings explored to the only purpose of plundering the "treasures" they contained, and then covered up or even destroyed to prevent others from appropriating paintings that had not been deemed worth the taking. Tunnels plumbing deep into the bowels of the earth in search of an ancient wall to perforate, to recover statues or other objects. A dismal, but true picture, which, however, needs to be reconsidered in the light of the culture of those times to be judged equitably.

In the first half of the 18th century, archaeological research was hardly a science, being generally regarded as a mere instrument for the collecting of antiquities and, hence, a pastime for wealthy aristocrats who could afford its costs, as well as an engrossing subject of conversation at parties. Even Winckelmann, the pioneer of scientific history of Classical art, who was highly critical of the excavations of the Vesuvian sites by the engineer corps, observed that the sappers' ignorance of the ancient world slowed down their work, as they did not know where to look for ancient works of art.

As regards excavation techniques, the methods used elsewhere were hardly more sophisticated. In fact, the solutions found by the investigators of the Vesuvian sites to deal first with the requirements of the excavation, and then with those of preservation and accessibility to visitors, were fundamental landmarks in the development of archaeology as a science and the

1. J.-L. Desprez,
Ceremony
in the Temple of Isis,
in Saint Non, Voyage
pittoresque, I, pl. 176

growth of an awareness of the significance of the archaeological heritage for society.

This process was stimulated, on the one hand, by the commitment with which the excavators set to this new task as soon as they began to grasp the significance of what they were discovering, on the other, by the enlightened patronage of Charles of Bourbon, who sensed that he needed to steer in a completely different direction an enterprise which had begun merely for the sake of dynastic glory.

Some of the innovations he fostered were crucial. Archaeological research, which had been the pursuit of refined aristocrats, became a state enterprise, for which the engineer corps of the army was deployed, and whose books were kept by the Ministers of the Kingdom. In 1755, Charles instituted the Accademia Ercolanense, charged with scientifically illustrating the monuments brought to light. When, in 1759, he quit Naples to rise to the throne of Spain with the name of Charles III, he took off a ring found in the Vesuvian excavations to stress that the ties connecting a people and a land to the vestiges of its history are unbreakable (although he was the one who had brought from Rome to Naples the collection of antiquities he had inherited from his mother, Elisabetta Farnese).

Even from Madrid, until 1776, i.e. as long as Bernardo Tanucci held the regency of the kingdom of Naples for young Ferdinand IV, Charles continued to follow the events of the excavation. In 1763, a royal rescript put an end to the shameful practice of demolition.

Initially, excavations were done haphazardly in several unrelated sites in the area where the first discoveries had been made, notably the complex of Julia Felix near the Amphitheater, the Villa of Cicero near Porta Ercolano, and the houses of *Regio* VIII. All these areas were subsequently covered up again.

In the Sixties and Seventies, instead, work concentrated on homogeneous groups of buildings which were left in sight. They included, in the area outside Porta Ercolano, several funerary monuments along Via dei Sepolcri, and the Villa of Diomedes; inside the walls, the House of the Surgeon and part of the *Insula occidentalis*. Some work was also done in the area of the Theaters, the Triangular Forum and the Temple of Isis.

In January 1799, the French army of General Championnet conquered Naples and proclaimed the short-lived Parthenopean Republic, which only lasted until June. Nevertheless, it was only a few years later that Ferdinand IV came back to Naples, to be deposed once again in 1806 by Joseph Bonaparte. The latter gave a renewed impulse to excavation, increasing personnel and employing soldiers as well. The work-force of Pompeii reached a peak of 688 civilians and 1,500 sappers under the reign of Joachim Murat, who took over the throne of Naples in 1808 when Joseph Bonaparte was made king of Spain. Murat's wife, Caroline, Napoleon's sister, was an enthusiastic sponsor of the excavations of Pompeii. She financed it with her own personal funds and backed a plan to gain an overall view of the extension of the city, hitherto unknown, by tracing the perimeter of the walls, expropriating the overlying plots. Caroline also contributed greatly to the diffusion of the results of the excavations by keeping an intense correspondence with personalities all over Europe and encouraging the printing of guidebooks with plans of the site. It is thanks to her munificence that Charles François Mazois could operate in Pompeii between 1809 and 1813, gathering material for his *Les ruines de Pompéi*, the *summa* on the excavations in the early Bourbon period.

The excavators

The official excavation of Pompeii (which at the time was confused with the nearby city of Stabiae), on the rise known as "collina della Civita", was begun on March 30th, 1748, by a few men led by Roque Joachim de Alcubierre, a colonel of the Bourbon engineer corps, the same man

who, in 1738, had dug tunnels to investigate Herculaneum, availing himself of soldiers, convicts and mines, and relying on the skill of Vesuvian well-diggers to recover paintings and statues from the bowels of the earth. In Pompeii, whose different mode of interment made excavation much easier, Alcubierre was assisted from 1750 to 1764 by the Swiss engineer Karl Weber who, on his own initiative, began to make drawings of what was being brought to light. In 1764, Weber's place was taken by Francesco La Vega, who eventually succeeded to Alcubierre, and remained director of the excavations until his death in 1780. Under La Vega, excavation was carried out on homogeneous, gradually expanding topographic nuclei, with the final aim of bridging the gaps between the different areas. The excavated buildings were left in sight, their paintings were documented, and the monuments were restored to make them accessible to an ever increasing public of visitors.

During the French occupation of 1799, General Championnet himself, a most learned man, ordered the immediate resumption of excavation, which had been interrupted for some time. Assisted by the Abbot Mattia Zarrilli, Championnet personally unearthed two houses, which were later named after him (VIII, 2, 1-3).

After his return to Naples in 1804, Ferdinand IV entrusted Pietro La Vega with recommencing the excavation of Pompeii. Pietro, the brother of Francesco, continued to direct the excavations even during the decade of Napoleonic rule, when work was resumed again in 1808, until 1814, when he was replaced by Antonio Bonucci. Under Joseph Bonaparte, the Minister himself, Cristoforo Saliceti, was charged with the supervision of the works. Saliceti excavated the House of Sallustius. The most remarkable personage of this period, however, was Michele Arditi, director of the Museum of Portici and superintendent of the excavations from 1807 to 1815, who continued to work in this capacity, together with Bonucci, during the second Bourbon period. Arditi freed the city from the piles of excavated earth. Above all, he drafted a plan for the expropriation of the area overlying the ancient city, once its perimeter had been identified, which was enacted mainly thanks to the enthusiasm of Queen Caroline. During the French decade, diggings were carried out to join the Theater area in the southern part of the city with the area of Porta Ercolano to the north. In the process, the Forum area was explored. Among the most remarkable discoveries of this period are the Basilica and the House of Pansa.

The urban development of Pompeii

Pompeii was founded – possibly as early as the end of the 7th century B.C. – on a rise formed by lava from a prehistoric eruption of the Vesuvius, in a dominant position along the coast, at the mouth of the river Sarno. The Etruscans certainly must have acted as catalysts for its foundation. From the beginning, the rise was protected by walls enclosing its whole area. Initially, however, the only areas with buildings were that of the future Forum of the Roman city (*Regio* VII), where a temple dedicated to Apollo was erected, and the area of the so-called Doric Temple, later occupied by the Triangular Forum (*Regio* VIII).

At the beginning of the Samnite period, the city extended moderately first east and then northwards into *Regio* VI. A major eastward expansion began around the end of the 3rd century B.C. Pompeii eventually came to occupy a surface of about 66 hectares comprising several public areas and buildings.

The city was laid out along two main east-west street axises, viz. that of Via delle Terme-Via della Fortuna-Via di Nola and that of Via Marina-Via dell'Abbondanza, intersected by the main north-south axis of Via Vesuvio-Via Stabiana.

Seven gates opened in the walls, from which issued roads connecting Pompeii to other cities, to the maritime district, and to the other districts of its hinterland. Its necropolises lay alongside these roads.

[A.V.]

2. C.H. Kniep,
*Marie Caroline visiting
the excavations of
Pompeii, 1808-1815*

ITINERARY OF THE NECROPOLIS OF PORTA ERCOLANO

ITINERARY OF THE VIA CONSOLARE

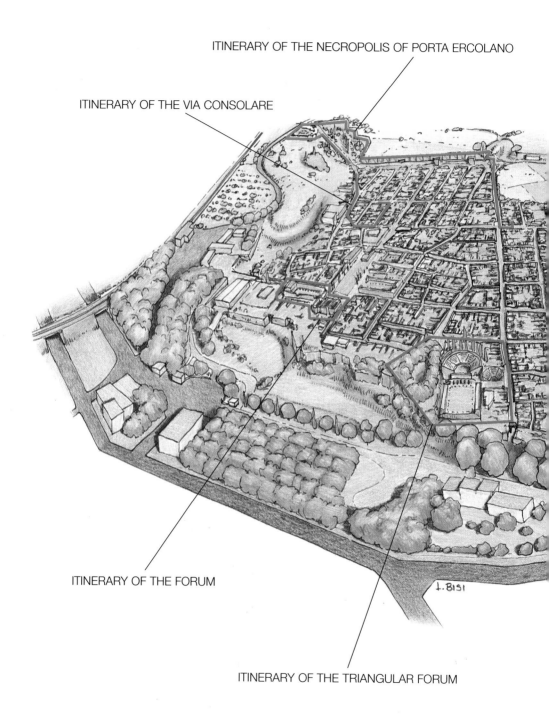

ITINERARY OF THE FORUM

ITINERARY OF THE TRIANGULAR FORUM

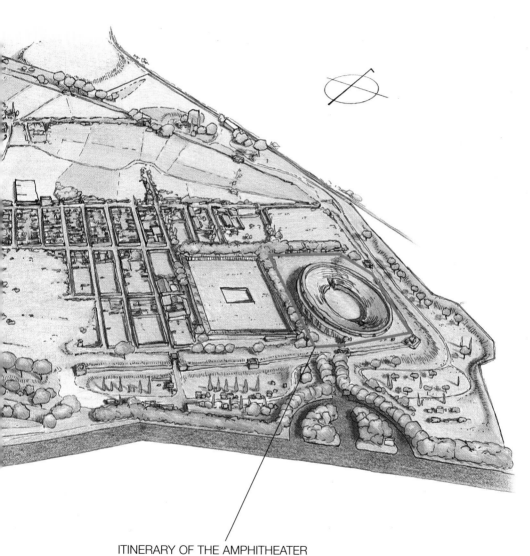

ITINERARY OF THE AMPHITHEATER

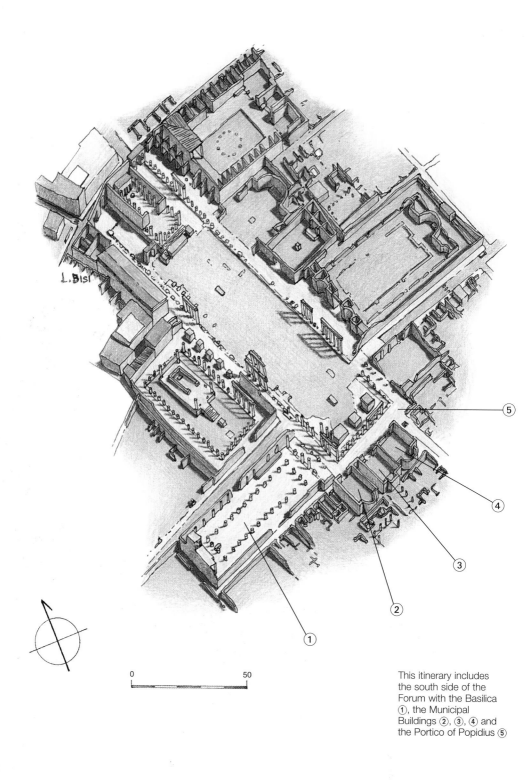

L. BISI

0 — 50

This itinerary includes
the south side of the
Forum with the Basilica
①, the Municipal
Buildings ②, ③, ④ and
the Portico of Popidius ⑤

The itinerary begins from the Forum, the great rectangular square which, from the beginning, was the focus of the political, administrative, religious, social and economic life of the city. Several important public buildings looked onto the Forum. On its north side, the square is dominated by the Capitolium, *the main temple of Pompeii, behind which rises the Vesuvius. Walking along the east side, north of Via dell'Abbondanza, one passes the* Macellum, *i.e. the fish and meat market, the Temple of the Public Lares, a temple dedicated to the Genius of the Emperor, and the Building of Eumachia, where business was transacted, and the corporation of the* fullones *had its seat.*

On the west side are the Forum olitorium, *i.e. the vegetable market, and the east side of the Temple of Apollo.*

South of the axis of Via dell'Abbondanza are the main administrative buildings.

[A.V.]

① **Basilica**
VIII, 1, 1
Date of excavation: 1813

The Basilica, lying at the southern extremity of the west side of the square, opens onto the Forum with an open-air vestibule whose five doorways lead to the main hall. There were secondary entrances in the long sides as well.

The name Basilica (in ancient Greek "house of the king") indicates the main function of this building, which was the palace of justice, and harks back to one of the prerogatives of the king in archaic times although, of course, the administration of justice in Roman cities was a prerogative of magistrates with jurisdictional powers, in Pompeii the *duoviri iure dicundo*. The imposing architecture of basilicas celebrates the solemnity of law, making them the most representative material embodiment of the State, and was used as a model by the Christians for their magnificent temples in honor of God.

The hall is divided into three naves by two rows of majestic columns on Attic bases, made of superimposed brick tiles cut and arranged to form grooves which, once the column was coated with stucco, imitated those of marble columns.

On the axis of the central nave, on the short side opposite the vestibule, stood the *tribunal*, i.e. the podium reserved to the magistrates, with its impressive double row of columns crowned by a tympanum.

The walls are graced by semicolumns also arranged in two rows, Ionic below, Corinthian above. The latter, which rose above the wall, attaining the same height as the columns of the portico, provided support for the single-truss roof and allowed light to penetrate from the space between the walls and the roof.

The Basilica, built around the last quarter of the 2nd century B.C., was also the main meeting place of the town, where one came to

3. F. Mazois, Reconstruction of the west wall of the Basilica seen from the inside (Mazois, III, pl. XVI)

hear the latest news, keep in touch with one's contacts, and make business. On the First Style decoration of the walls, an extraordinary number of graffiti of all sorts, left by the frequenters of the building, were found. Even some Pompeians seem to have thought that the practice had got a bit out of hand, as one of the graffiti reads: "I am amazed, oh wall, that you have not yet collapsed under the weight of the inanities of so many scribblers."
[A.V.]

4. F. Mazois,
View of the east entrance
to the Basilica
(Mazois, III, pl. XVII)

Pictorial decoration

The abundance of documentation offered by Pompeii enabled August Mau, in the last century, to subdivide its pictorial wall decoration into four styles corresponding to as many periods.
The **First Style**, also called "structural style", is the international artistic language of the Hellenistic world. It is found in Pompeii from the 3rd century to the end of the Samnite age. It hid the actual masonry of the wall under an in-relief and painted stucco facing reproducing a wall of large, accurately arranged squared blocks which were soon decorated in imitation of the different qualities of marble of rich Hellenistic houses, impossible to find in Italy. The colors and veins of the marble were combined in a geometric pattern representing large orthostats alternating with horizontal courses of isodomic rectangular blocks above a dark socle. Above the blocks, the wall was crowned by a white stucco cornice. If the wall was very high, it was completed with a false veranda subdivided by pilasters or stucco semi-columns. This painted stucco decoration enhances the loftiness of the room and employs pictorial illusion to expand the space of the room's true architecture.
The **Second Style**, introduced in Pompeii by the Roman colonists, remained in vogue until the beginning of the Augustan age.
Developing further the concept of the First Style, it gives up relief, creating by solely pictorial means a scenography that cancels the wall by giving the illusion of extending beyond it, composed of columns, porticoes, shrines, foreshortened views of buildings, and theater wings, animated by human figures or vignettes. Sometimes it features representations of theater stages with life-size figures of the players. Soon, however, the "illusory realism" of the painted architectural structures evolved into a further expansion of the actual space of the room. Thus, the wall "opens up", showing, through openings in the structures in the foreground, perspective renderings of buildings set in faraway landscapes.
The **Third Style**, characteristic of all the early Imperial age until the time of Claudius, is the final result of the Second Style's tendency to depart from the realism of architectural representation in the last years of the Republican period. In this new style the structures occupy a pictorial space which has lost its contact with reality. The wall, formerly canceled by the illusion of depth, has become the space where an array of sometimes miniature ornaments and fantastic figures are deployed. Freed from the slavish imitation of architecture, columns become vegetable stalks or candelabra, and the spaces are arranged hierarchically. The subdivision of the wall in a socle, middle zone and upper zone now becomes a conventional pattern in which each area is developed independently, although with some occasional overlapping. The architecture of the middle zone, which is the most conspicuous, converges towards a central shrine framing a large picture (generally a mythological scene) acting as the focus of the whole composition. At the sides of the shrine, the wall is partitioned in monochrome panels separated by tenuous decorative motifs. At the center of these panels are vignettes with figures or landscapes. In the upper zone the architecture becomes miniaturized and is combined with vegetable arabesques, and small landscapes or still lifes alternate with masks and fantastic figures.
In the **Fourth Style**, which already appears under Claudius, but takes hold especially after the earthquake of 62 A.D., the trend of the final phase of the Third Style to increasingly complex ornamentation and a loss of an overall compositional logic is enhanced and brought to maturation. The side panels of the middle zone of the walls are often "opened up" to reveal perspective views of architectural structures that draw the gaze of the observer beyond the wall, although they lack the realism of the Second Style. Colors become brighter and the chromatic contrast between the different sections of the wall, formerly based on the rhythmic alternation of two background colors, evolves into sometimes lurid polychromy. Ornamental motifs are crowded together and superimposed. The panels imitate tapestries at the center of which are figures suspended in flight or looking out from medallions, genre scenes, or landscapes. Pictures and vignettes now are painted in a fluid, "impressionistic" style, with a skilful use of shading to enhance the volume of the bodies and spotted highlights to accentuate the illusion of depth. Within the framework of this general style, very diverse compositional systems were employed, some so redundant they could be categorized as "baroque", others featuring a simple subdivision in panels of various colors with, at the center, vignettes with stereotypical motifs. Occasionally, mythological or hunting scenes take up a whole wall. There is also a renewed interest in relief stucco decoration, often polychrome and graced by lively tridimensional ornaments.
[A.V.]

②, ③, ④ Municipal Buildings
VIII, 2, 6-10
Date of excavation: 1814

The south side of the Forum was taken up by three municipal buildings which, being connected to the west with the Basilica and to the east with the *Comitium*, delimited a space entirely devoted to the administration of the city, completed, beyond the portico, in the open air part of the square, by a number of honorary bases, arches and pedestals for statues of the members of the imperial family and eminent citizens.

The municipal buildings were not built according to a single consistent plan, and not even in the same period. The ones on the east side, although both date from precolonial times, and are symmetrically arranged at the sides of the longitudinal axis of the Forum, are not aligned. The westernmost building, instead, is a more recent addition. All three consist of large rectangular halls – with apses in the side buildings, a large rectangular niche in the central one – and show substantial brickwork rebuilding following the earthquake of 62 A.D. The lavish marble pave-

ment of the western building was found still *in situ*.
The specific function of each building is debated. The traditional view that they were the rooms of the *aediles*, the *decuriones* and the *duoviri* is not quite convincing. It is more plausible to regard the east building ④ as the hall of the magistrates, the central one ③, whose walls are covered with niches, as the *tabularium*, i.e. the archive where the city laws were kept, and the west one ② as the hall of the decurions.
[A.V.]

5. F. Mazois,
*View of the east side
of the Forum in 1814
(Mazois, III, pl. XXIX)*

⑤ **Portico of Popidius**
Date of excavation: 1814

A tuff portico, connected by a double nave to the Forum-side façade of the *Comitium* and to those of the municipal buildings, ran along three sides of the square. It was built by Vibius Popidius even earlier than the foundation of the Roman colony. He imparted a monumental appearance to the south side of the Forum and provided an architectural connection for the buildings opening onto the Forum, which had been built at different times and with different alignments. This colonnade was greatly restructured under the Empire, when travertine columns were progressively erected on the east side of the square to create vestibules for the new buildings. Travertine columns replaced the earlier tuff ones on the west side, where the portico had two superimposed rows of columns, Doric below, Ionic above, as it was surmounted by a gallery reachable by a staircase placed beside the Basilica. The original tuff paving stones of the Forum were also replaced by travertine stones.
[A.V.]

Political and administrative life

The three main political and administrative institutions of Pompeii were the *ordo decurionum*, the magistrates, and the *populus.* The first was the town council, endowed with legislative and administrative powers. Magistrates represented the executive power. There were four, grouped in two pairs. The *duoviri iure dicundo*, of higher rank, were the supreme representatives of the city. They called the assemblies of the people and of the Council, made public and enacted the decrees of the decurions, supervised the aerarium and managed the economy and finances of the city. Above all, they administered justice. The *aediles*, the subordinates of the *duoviri*, were generally young men on their first public assignment and hence concerned with giving a good impression. Their tasks included the maintenance of the streets and the sacred and civil public buildings, assuring a regular supply of water and food, giving out rations, police surveillance and, in general, seeing to all the practical needs of city life. The magistrates were elected annually. After finishing their year of office they became members for life of the Council of the decurions, which thus granted the continuity of urban administration and was the seat of the local aristocracies. The *duoviri* elected at the end of each five-year period, called *quinquennales*, had further important powers: they were charged not only with investigating the administrative and fiscal position of every citizen, but also with verifying if the individual decurions still had the wealth, morality and other assets required of the members of the Council, or should, instead, be dismissed. They also had the prerogative of admitting new members, not elected by the people, to the *ordo* when there were some gaps to be filled, thus making them eligible as magistrates in future elections. The *quinquennales* were always members of the same few families controlling the electorate through a network of political allegiances. As to the *populus*, i.e. the assembly of the citizens with right to vote, their primary function was to elect the magistrates and formally ratify the resolutions of the Council. The candidates possessing the necessary prerequisites stood on the *suggestum*, the orators' tribune, dressed in a white (in latin *candida*) tunic, and expounded their political program to the *populus*. Quite often there were electoral allegiances between candidates. Only free-born male citizens had the right to vote, but women, slaves and other persons without the right to vote also joined in the tough electoral competition taking place every spring, when the streets filled up with colorful electoral inscriptions. The winners of the elections had to sponsor public building works or games and pay the staff of the town administration at their own expense.
[A.V.]

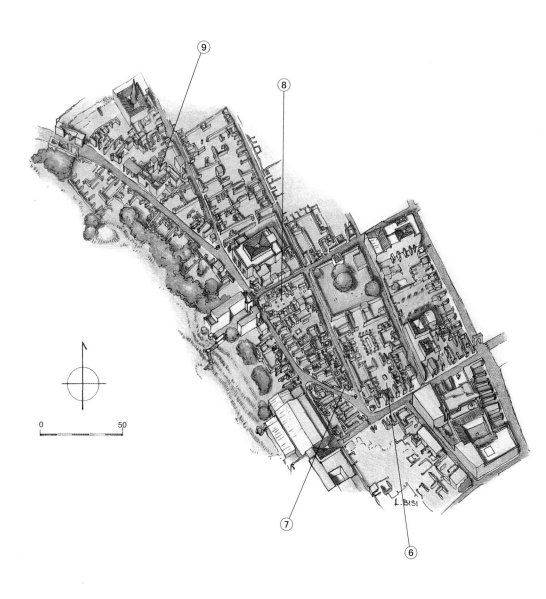

0   50

L. BISI

This itinerary comprises the House of Pansa ⑥, the *Thermopolium* of Fortunata ⑦, the House of the Baker ⑧, and the House of the Surgeon ⑨

Most of the itinerary runs along the Via Consolare, on which open some very interesting old and lavishly decorated private houses ⑥, ⑨ as well as workshops and stores ⑦, ⑧. [F.P.]

⑥ House of Pansa
(House of Gnaeus Alleius
Nigidius Maius; *Insula
Arriana Polliana*)
VI, 6, 1
Dates of excavation: 1810, 1813-1815, 1824-1825, 1827, 1898, 1901; 1943 (stratigraphic excavation)

In 19th-century descriptions this dwelling, like the nearby houses of the Faun and the Labyrinth, is regarded as an ideal example of the Roman and Italic aristocratic *domus*, where the rooms are symmetrically arranged around the atrium and peristyle. Excavations done in the 1940s and recent studies of the architecture of the house have established that it was built around the middle of the 2nd century B.C. in the place of pre-existing private buildings, bringing several workshops and living quarters together in a single complex.
At the time of the eruption only some small portions of the *insula*, such as the two

bakeries opening onto the Vico di Modesto and the Vico della Fullonica, were independent from the house. Shortly before the eruption, an extensive area behind the peristyle had also been incorporated and was used as a garden (this area is presently not accessible, as it houses an experimental plant nursery). At the center of the tuff *opus quadratum* façade, in which six *tabernae* open, is the monumental vestibule of the house, framed by two half-pillars surmounted by exquisite capitals of the so-called "sofa" type. Behind it is the corridor (*fauces*) leading to the atrium. Little remains of its pavement; according to 19th-century descriptions, here was a welcome inscription (*salve*) inserted within a mosaic which was later removed and taken to the Naples archaeological museum.
Around the atrium, at whose center is a marble impluvium of the Augustan age, are several rooms. Some still have the original floors made at

the time of the construction of the house, e.g. the third cubiculum to the right, which has a *cocciopesto* floor (small earthenware fragments mixed with mortar), half of which is decorated with a lozenge pattern, while the other half, where the bed stood, was left undecorated. The doorsteps of the *cocciopesto* floors of the two *alae*, placed one at each end of the long sides of the atrium, were decorated with swastikas and squares.
The only preserved mosaic graces the *tablinum*, i.e. the large formal sitting room opposite the entrance; it is white, with a thick black stripe running along the edge.
The great peristyle has 17 tuff Ionic columns which were stuccoed in Imperial times. Around it opened the most representative rooms of the house, including a huge hall (*oecus*). There is also a great pool – built in the Augustan age to replace an earlier compluvium – in which a painting

6. Reconstruction of the interior of the House of Pansa (W. Gell, J. P. Gandy, pl. 36)

representing fish was seen when it was excavated.

As an inscription on the outside of the house tells us, at the time of the eruption of 79 A.D. the house was being renovated. Many of the walls still lacked their new frescoes. Only the great cubiculum on the left side of the peristyle still featured a painting (completely vanished today) dating back to the time of Augustus.

During the renovation, some valuable pieces of the furniture of the house were stored in the garden, carefully wrapped in linen cloths. They included a small bronze group of Dionysus with a Satyr, and a three-lamp candelabrum, also of bronze, decorated with a statuette of Dionysus riding a panther.

[F. P.]

The painted inscriptions of the House of Pansa

A glass over the fifth block of entrance No. 3 on Via delle Terme signals the presence of an Oscan epigraph, one of seven inscriptions called "*eítuns*" after the verbal form found in every one of them. These inscriptions marked the gathering points of the town militia for the defense of the walls at the time of Sulla's siege in 89 B.C.
Eksuk amvíanud eítuns/ anter tiurrí XII íní ver(u)/ Saprínu, puf faamat/ M(a)r(as) Aadíriis V(ibieís)
"By this crossroads (alley) those who go between the XII tower and the Salt Gates, where Maras Adirius, the son of Vibius, is in command."

On the jamb of the entrance of shop No. 19 was a long inscription advertising the putting up for rent of some rooms and shops in the period immediately preceding the eruption. "From the 1st of July, in the *Insula Arriana Polliana,* now belonging to Gnaeus Alleius Nigidius Maius, shops with habitable second floors (*tabernae cum pergulis*), luxury apartments (*cenacula equestria*) and houses (*domus*). Apply to Primus, the servant of Gnaeus Alleius Nigidius Maius."
[F. P.]

7. F. Duban, Frescoes in the House of Pansa, 1823-1828

8. Bronze group of Dionysus and a Satyr, from the House of Pansa. Naples, Museo Archeologico Nazionale

⑦ *Thermopolium* or *caupona* of Fortunata (Tavern of Fortunata)
VI, 3, 17-20
Date of excavation: 1806

The *thermopolium* is called "of Fortunata" from the female name read in an electoral inscription in support of Marcus Casellius Marcellus, a candidate to aedileship in 79 A.D. (*Marcellum Fortunata cupit*), written on the wall plaster on the left jamb of the entrance.

At entrance No. 20 stands a large counter faced with marble, containing four large earthenware jars for wine or warm drinks.

Against the right wall was the cooking plate on which food was cooked or heated. For the most demanding customers there were some rooms at Nos. 16-19, and possibly also other rooms on the second floor, reached by means of a wooden staircase whose base is still partially visible in the triangular room at No. 18.

Almost in front of the entrance of the *thermopolium*, at the crossroads between the Via Consolare and the Vico di Modesto, is one of the forty public fountains of Pompeii found up to now.

The water collector is formed of four trachyte slabs joined by iron cramps. The perforated pillar from which the water pipe issued is decorated with a very rough bas-relief representing an eagle clutching a hare in its claws.
[F. P.]

⑧ House of the Baker
VI, 3, 3
Dates of excavation: 1809-1810

The ground floor of this old atrium house with a garden at the back was entirely taken up, after the earthquake of 62 A.D., by a bakery (one of the largest of the 35 documented up to now in Pompeii), while the living quarters were moved to the second floor. The house was built in the 2nd century B.C. Structures dating from this period include the tuff impluvium, the earthenware well curb graced with female heads, and the *cocciopesto* floors of the rooms lying on the long sides and the back of the atrium, respectively identifiable as *cubicula* and the *tablinum*; no traces remain today of these floors and of the white and black mosaic, dating from the last years of the 1st century B.C., seen by the first visitors of the house in a room right of the *tablinum*.

Already at the entrance there are evident signs that the house was transformed into a workshop. The jambs of the doorways of the two shops (Nos. 1 and 4, each with its own independent living quarters) and those of the entrance

*10. F. Mazois,
Reconstruction in
cross-section of the House
of the Baker
(Mazois, II, pl. XIX)*

*9. F. Mazois,
Reconstruction of a
thermopolium
(Mazois, II, pl. VIII, 1)*

*11. F. Mazois,
View of the House of the
Baker (Mazois, II,
pl. XVIII, 2)*

to the upper floor (No. 2) were entirely rebuilt in *opus latericium* (brickwork), a type of masonry which was widely used in Pompeii for post-earthquake reconstruction. Inside, all the entrances to the rooms opening onto the atrium were rebuilt, and four brick pillars were erected at the corners of the old impluvium to reinforce the roof and allow the construction of a gallery giving access to the rooms on the upper floor. A staircase immediately to the right of the entrance to the atrium led up to these rooms. Apparently, the renovation of the house was not yet complete at the time of the eruption, as the old lava doorsteps were being replaced with travertine ones (a large block that was to be hewn into a doorstep lies against the wall on the left of the atrium). From the excavation reports and the notes left by the first investigators of this building – which remained for a long time the only bakery found in Pompeii – we known that most of the rooms opening onto the atrium were being used as storerooms. More specifically, in the first cubiculum on the right were found numerous amphorae containing different types of flour.

The most interesting sector of the entire complex is the old garden (*hortus*) of the house, where the equipment for grinding grain and preparing and cooking bread was installed. Immediately behind the wall of the tablinum, beside the mouth of a tank, are two small water basins. Near them, as a 19th-century watercolor attests, was a fresco on two registers, depicting Vesta above, flanked by the Lares, and two snakes (symbols of the *Genius loci*) below, advancing towards an altar loaded with offerings. On the right is the great vaulted oven, whose mouth is framed by a lintel and jambs made of trachytic lava. In the open garden, which had an independent entrance from the Vico di Modesto, are four trachytic lava millstones supported by an *opus incertum* base. They are arranged in two staggered rows to take up as little room as possible. Around their base the floor was paved with trachyte stones to preserve it from the hooves of the animals used to turn the millstones. The great open room on the right, where stone supports for a great table were seen, was used to leave the bread to rise before it was put into the oven. The room on the left of the tablinum, where one entered by a narrow doorway, was the kitchen, whose cooking bench is partially preserved. The last room of the bakery was connected both with the garden and the Vico di Modesto. The manger leaning against the wall opposite the entrance indicates it was the stable. F. Mazois reports that the skeleton of a mule with its harness was found here.

[F. P.]

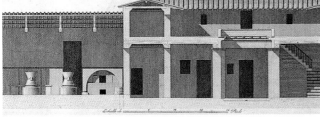

The bakeries of Pompeii

"Bakeries, at least in Pompeii, were also mills (*pistrinum et panificium*). The shop where bread was sold was provided with lava millstones, a work-room where the dough was prepared, and an oven. All Pompeian millstones are identical. They are hewn from hard lava, and consist of three parts: a fixed, bell-shaped element, the *meta*, surrounded by a masonry base fitted with a metal lamina to collect the flour; on the *meta* was placed the *catillus*, a moving element with a double truncated-cone shape whose upper part served as a funnel wherein the grain was poured, while the lower part ground the grain by revolving against the sides of the *meta* (total height 1.40-1.70 meters). To allow the grain to penetrate between the two elements and avoid excessive friction, the *catillus* was slightly lifted from the *meta* by a vertical wooden beam connected to a frame. This contraption was attached to a pack animal, normally a donkey (hence the name "*mola asinaria*"). The use of animals (which were kept in the stable during the night) required the millstones to be installed in an open space, and a stone pavement to be laid around each to keep the animals from ruining the packed earth or *opus signinum* floor by continuously treading upon it. Very often the oven (*furnus*) was installed in the same open space, near the work-room, and sometimes communicating with it by a small door opening onto the platform in front of the mouth of the oven. [...] There were about thirty mills in Pompeii, a proof of the importance of the various kinds of flour used to prepare meal and loaves, the main food of agricultural workers. [...] From the Augustan age onward, one cooked a type of bread often shaped as a circular loaf with cuts dividing it into sections; today, one still finds forms very similar to those found in Pompeii and Herculaneum. The bread was baked as follows. The fire was lit in the oven with vine faggots (the most common Pompeian fuel). The smoke went out through the chimney installed in front of the mouth, sometimes ending in *tubuli*. The fire was kept going until the bricks of the vault became white with heat. It takes an hour and a half to heat a rural oven with a diameter of 2 meters. In the meanwhile the dough, after being left to rest, wrapped in a cloth, in a kneading trough placed in the work-room, was shaped into loaves ready to be put into the oven when it was hot enough. At this point, the ashes and cinders were removed and stored in a *dolium* for further use as wood coal. The oven was cleaned with a sorghum broom or with rags drenched in a vessel filled with water (a jar or a lava basin placed at the foot of the oven). Then the bread was put into the oven with a wooden shovel, and the oven was closed with an iron shutter fitted with a sliding panel to regulate the temperature. It takes 30-45 minutes to cook the bread, which was taken out with an iron shovel."
(From J.-P. Adam, *La construction romaine. Matériaux et techniques*, Picard, Paris 1984)

12. Reconstruction of the bakery of Terentius Proculus (VII, 2, 3)

⑨ House of the Surgeon

VI, 1, 9-10 and 23
Dates of excavation:
1770-1771, 1777; 1926
(stratigraphic excavation)

The house stands out from the other buildings looking onto this stretch of the Via Consolare, as its façade is higher and built of regular limestone blocks. As the same masonry is used for many of the inside walls, this house was long regarded as a primary source for our knowledge of the most ancient Roman and Italic houses, and a date as early as the 5th century B.C. was proposed for it. Limited soundings carried out in the Twenties revealed that the presently visible structures are the result of two renovations of the Samnite age which, as in other documented cases (Houses of the Faun, of the Diadumenoi and of the Centaur), involved a considerable rise of the floor level. A recent study of the excavations data has shown that, from the beginning, the house had an impluvium at the center of the atrium, and hence it must have been built much more recently than one had thought, sometime in the 3rd century B.C. The house has a regular plan, with the most important rooms arranged around the atrium. The decoration described by the first excavators is preserved only in some points. The doorstep of the left *ala* is enhanced by an exquisite coffered motif datable to the early Empire. A very interesting room with a window opens onto the small garden (*hortus*) at the back of the house: its external wall is decorated with a First Style painting datable to the 2nd century B.C., which was notched all over to allow a new layer of white plaster to adhere; inside, it is decorated with a Fourth Style painting made shortly after the middle of the 1st century A.D. The floor, made of

13. F. Mazois,
*View of the
Via Consolare
(Mazois, II, pl. II)*

pottery and travertine fragments, dates back to the Samnite age. At the center of the right hand wall is an almost vanished vignette depicting a poet. On the wall opposite the entrance a Hellenistic style painting was detached, probably representing a woman painter drawing a herm, assisted by a servant and sternly observed by three women. Below this vignette, two of the first visitors incised in the plaster a reminder of their passage. The first one, named Tullio, visited the house in 1799, while a second, anonymous visitor added the date of 1802. The conventional name of the house is due to the discovery here of more than forty surgical instruments, including some scalpels and several types of probes.
[F. P.]

Surgical instruments

The discovery of surgical instruments in a house caused a great sensation. The scholar Domenico Romanelli described it thus: *"Through these finds, one has finally learned that the ancient surgical art had many ingenuous resources to relieve the sufferings of humanity. Up to now, it was thought to be rudimentary, and one could not understand some passages of ancient authors discussing it. [...] All these instruments are of the purest copper, with bronze handles, and most have been found in sheaths also made of copper, or of boxwood."* The surprise of Romanelli's contemporaries was great, because one had long speculated on the skill of Roman surgeons, and the discovery certainly bore witness to a far greater knowledge than one had supposed. For example, the instruments included a cleverly designed cupping glass for blood-letting. It consisted of a copper hemisphere with four holes which were stopped with clay. It was applied to the skin and then heated to create a vacuum that increased the bleeding. To detach it, the holes were opened. Some objects found later were even more astounding, e.g. some gynaecological retractors perfectly identical to those used today. The complexity of these tools and the modernity of their forms are evidence of an advanced surgery, assisted by a medicine combining popular lore with an appropriate use of substances whose effectiveness is still recognized today by official pharmacopoeia. These substances were taken from the mineral and animal worlds as well as the vegetable one. While some are still used today, e.g. cod-liver oil, digitalis, or iron, the use of others strikes us as decidedly bizarre. For example, a brew of Herculaneum ants was regarded as an excellent disinfectant, as those ants were considered to be unusually large. It is true that ants produce formic acid, a well-known disinfectant. It remains to be seen whether in Herculaneum there actually existed a subspecies which was larger than normal and, thus, capable of producing more formic acid. At any rate, this belief had some truth in it, as it arose from empirical experimentation whose results were handed down from one generation to another.
[A.C.]

14. "Paintress" at work, fresco from the House of the Surgeon. Naples, Museo Archeologico Nazionale

ITINERARY OF THE NECROPOLIS OF PORTA ERCOLANO

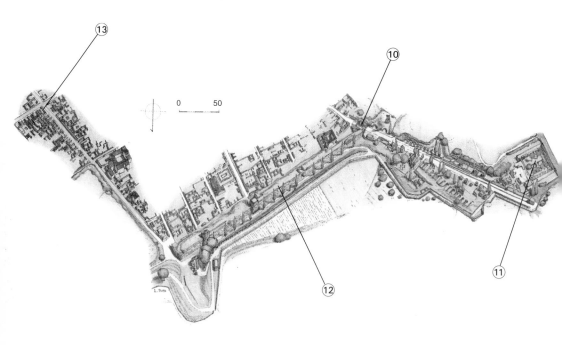

This itinerary comprises the Necropolis outside Porta Ercolano (10), the Villa of Diomedes (11), the north stretch of the city walls (12), and the area of the crossroads of Orpheus (13) where the exploration of Pompeii began

Going out of the city through the Porta Ercolano (whose ancient name was Veru Sarinu or Porta Saliniensis, because it was oriented towards salt mines lying outside the city), one walks along the Via delle Tombe ("Road of the Tombs", a modern name alluding to the numerous funerary monuments flanking it) leading to Oplontis, Herculaneum and Naples. Several important suburban villas open onto this road, including the villa of the Mosaic Columns, only partially excavated; the villa "of Cicero", brought to light and then immediately covered up again in Bourbon times; the villa "of Diomedes". The tombs, dated between the middle of the 1st century B.C. and the Seventies of the 1st century A.D., provide an excellent sample of Roman funerary architecture. One then walks along the north stretch of the town walls, from Porta Ercolano to Tower XI, excavated during the French period, and finally re-enters the city through Porta Vesuvio.

[A. d'A.]

Vue des fouilles du côté de la porte de la Ville

15. F. Mazois,
View of the Porta
Ercolano from
the Via dei Sepolcri
(Mazois, I, pl. II)

Vue des nouvelles découvertes faites dans le fauboury occidental de Pompei

Necropolis of Porta Ercolano

(Via dei Sepolcri)
Dates of excavation:
1763-1814;
the excavation was
completed in 1834

As usual in Roman necropolises, the tombs are arranged along an important road just outside the city, in this case the one going north towards Herculaneum. Thus, the deceased – whose name was carved in a funerary epigraph – made sure he would be remembered by many for a long time. The law forbade burial inside the city and prescribed that a strip along the city walls should be free of constructions. This public soil, however, was often, as in this case, occupied by tombs, with the consent of the decurions (the town Senate), who issued decrees making an exception for citizens of special merit. The necropolis was one of the first areas of the city to be excavated. For a long time, it was the beginning and one of the highlights of the visit, an inexhaustible source of inspiration for countless drawings and watercolors by landscape painters and travelers.

The numerous tombs lined up along the road, interspersed by rows of shops and three suburban villas (of Cicero, of the Mosaic Columns, and of Diomedes), comprise most types of funerary monument found in Pompeii. One of the most conspicuous ones is the semicircular seat monument (*schola*) on the south side, datable to the late Augustan or Tiberian age. It belongs to the public priestess Mamia, who is commemorated by the inscription on the back of the seat. This type of monument which, in the case of the Pompeian examples, almost always belongs to a former *duovir* or a priestess, derives from the Greek honorary exedra. It was often completed by a column with a marble urn at the top, erected behind the seat.

Behind the tomb of Mamia is the tomb of the *Istacidii*, a well-know family of the Augustan age, excavated in 1828. It consists of a burial chamber decorated externally by semicolumns and surmounted by a partially reconstructed circular aedicule (*tholos*) which must have been graced by funerary statues. Inside the chamber, as usual, are a series of small niches in which the urns were walled in. The building can be dated to the second quarter of the 1st century B.C.

A little further, on the opposite side, is a Late Republican tomb called "of the Wreaths" after the decorative motif sculpted on its sides. As in the preceding tomb, the basement is surmounted by an aedicule for funerary statues, but in this case rectangular. Part of the architectural decoration of the aedicule, graced with spires and relief coffers, lies at the foot of the monument.

The following tomb is only partially preserved. Allegedly, the famous "blue vase" was found here. It is a glass amphora with a cameo white-on-blue representation of *amorini* harvesting grapes.

The following tomb, an unusual mixture of the "*schola*" and "niche" types, still unfinished in 79 A.D., may have belonged to the owners of the adjoining Villa of the Mosaic Columns.

Continuing along the south side, there are some "altar" tombs, which take their name from the altar crowning the basement containing the funerary chamber. The first has lost its marble facing, except for the epigraph commemorating its owner, Umbricius Scaurus, a well-known producer of *garum*, a very widely used fish-sauce. The marble facing of the following tomb (of Calventius Quietus and Naevoleia Tyche), instead, is almost completely preserved. The monument of Calventius bears representations of the *corona civica* and the *bisellium*. The former, a symbol of imperial power, possibly alludes to Calventius' office of *augustalis*, to which one acceded only by imperial nomination. The latter commemorates the conferring to the deceased of the honor of a front-row seat in the theater, also mentioned in the epigraph. On the tomb of Naevoleia and Munatius Faustus, along with the *bisellium* and a small portrait of the deceased woman, a cargo ship is depicted, regarded by some as a symbol of the soul sailing away towards the Beyond, but more probably alluding to Munatius' commercial activities. Both of the buildings are datable between 60 and 79 A.D.

[A.d'A.]

16. F. Mazois,
View of the
Via dei Sepolcri
(Mazois, I, pl. XIV)

17. View of the west side
of the Via dei Sepolcri

The cult of the dead

Until the 1st century A.D., the Romans cremated their dead. The ashes of the deceased were collected in earthenware, glass or, exceptionally, marble vases which were buried inside the enclosure surrounding the tomb or walled into the niches lining the walls of the funerary chamber. These urns, especially the glass ones, were sometimes placed inside a lead vessel for protection. When the urn was placed underground, the burial spot was generally indicated by stone or marble markers (*columella*) roughly reproducing a human bust, bearing a carved epigraph commemorating the deceased. In the urn one often placed a coin so that the deceased could pay Charon for ferrying him across the Acheron. There was often a hole connecting the urn to the surface, allowing the deceased to receive the libations offered during funerary ceremonies. When the burial ritual had been carried out, a banquet (*silicernium*) took place near the tomb, part of which was offered to the deceased. When the banquet was over, a mourning period of nine days (*novemdial*) began, at the end of which offerings were brought to the dead, and another banquet (*coena novemdialis*) was held, during which one ate the same food as in the *silicernium* (eggs, vegetables, lentils, broad beans, fowls). The official feasts of the dead were the *Feralia*, celebrated in February, which lasted nine days and were concluded, on February 21st, by the *Parentalia*, also involving a meal in honor of the dead. *Parentalia* was also the name of the feasts celebrated on the anniversary of the death of a member of one's family. In this case too, a funerary banquet was held, during which, among other things, broad beans were consumed, which had the power of protecting against the harm that the shadows of the dead could cause if they returned to earth. [A. d'A.]

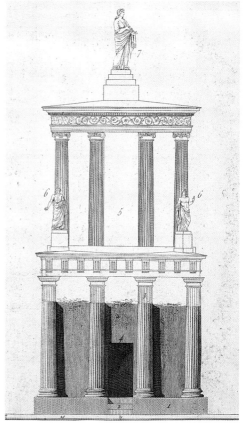

18. View of the Tomb of Mamia and the Istacidii

19. G.B. Piranesi, Reconstruction of the Tomb of the Istacidii

20. Narcissus, fresco from the Villa of Diomedes. Naples, Museo Archeologico Nazionale

21. J.-L. Desprez, Reconstruction of the Villa of Diomedes, in Saint-Non, Voyage pittoresque, I, pl. 184

⑪ Villa of Diomedes
(Via dei Sepolcri, 24)
Dates of excavation:
1771-1774

The entrance to this suburban building is on the Via dei Sepolcri, at a short distance from Porta Ercolano. Its incorrect attribution is due to the presence of the tomb of Marcus Arrius Diomedes on the opposite side of the road. The villa, built during the 2nd century B.C., was partially demolished to make room for the road after 80 B.C., the year when the Sullan colony was installed, with the consequent loss of prestige of the old Pompeian aristocracy.

A short staircase leads up to a prothyrum entrance opening directly onto the peristyle. Immediately left of the entrance is a triangular space occupied by the thermal sector, with a small portico, a *frigidarium* basin, a *tepidarium* and a *calidarium*. This thermal area comprises a kitchen, also triangular in plan. On the south side of the peristyle is a monumental cubiculum with an apse and three windows, probably for the *dominus*, preceded by another room adjoined by a small sleeping room. The west side is partially taken up by the tablinum, through which one reaches a gallery and then an ample triclinium with a view of the seaside. This triclinium rises above a great garden enclosed by a peristyle and supported by a square cryptoporticus. A staircase leads down to the garden, where one finds a fountain and a summer triclinium. The cryptoporticus, also used as a cellar, has an exit on the west side.

Inside the cryptoporticus the bodies of several people were found. They had sought refuge there, bringing with them jewels and coins, in a vain attempt to save themselves from the eruption.

The most striking characteristic of the building is its elaborate structure. The builders took advantage of the slope of the ground to distribute the villa on two levels, an arrangement that was well suited to a luxurious residence.

As in other suburban Pompeian villas, while the room-types (peristyle, baths, triclinia, sleeping rooms etc.) are those typical of every Roman house of a certain wealth, they are not arranged according to a standard plan, but rather freely, to suit the needs of the owner.

[L. F.]

Vue d'une Maison de Campagne située près de l'ancienne Ville de Pompeii: Rétablie et dessinée d'après sa forme actuelle et une partie des Colonnes encore existantes, ainsi qu'on présume qu'elle pouvoit être lors de sa destruction par la fameuse eruption du Vésuve arrivée le 24 Aout 79.

22. Dioskourides,
Itinerant musicians,
mosaic from the Villa of
Cicero. Naples, Museo
Archeologico Nazionale

23. Dioskourides,
The consulting of the
sorceress, mosaic from
the Villa of Cicero.
Naples, Museo
Archeologico Nazionale

24. Centaurs and
fantastic figures, fresco
from the Villa of Cicero.
Naples, Museo
Archeologico Nazionale

25. Rope-walking satyrs,
fresco from the
Villa of Cicero.
Naples, Museo
Archeologico Nazionale

The suburban villas of Pompeii

The suburban villas lying along the road which, going out of Porta Ercolano, connected Pompeii to the towns of the coast, reaching as far as Naples, were magnificent luxury residences belonging to members of the old Pompeian aristocracy. They are earlier than the road itself, which was built after 80 B.C., and some of them, as their orientation shows, were partially demolished to make room for its construction, a clear sign that the old Pompeian ruling class lost its prestige after the Sullan colony was founded. There were villas scattered all over the vast Pompeian suburb, both north and south of the city. Those lying along the coast were mostly residential, e.g. the magnificent Villa of Poppaea at Oplontis, which was a dependency of Pompeii, although it had a small urban center with a network of streets, as at Stabiae. There were coastal villas – also called "maritime" or "otium" – all along the Campanian littoral, from Misenum to Sorrento. Their density was such that the geographer Strabo observes they gave the impression of a single city. The beauty of the coast and the healthiness of its climate made it a choice destination for Roman aristocrats, who came here to rest the mind and the body. The villas of the productive type ("rustic" villas), instead, lay especially inland, in hilly areas where there was room for cultivation and pastures. Although they were equipped for the production of wine, oil, and cereals, as well as other agricultural products such as fruit, sometimes they also had exquisitely

frescoed luxury quarters where the owner of the *fundus* resided on and off to supervise work and to take a vacation away from city life. The most remarkable of the suburban villas outside Pompeii are certainly the Villa of Diomedes and the Villa of the Mysteries, the first for its being built on two levels, the second for its famous Second Style paintings.
The only partially excavated Villa of the Mosaic Columns is also

interesting. It has a large garden with a fountain faced with seashells and a mosaic made of glaze tesserae. At the center of this *viridarium*, four columns, also faced with polychrome mosaic, presently in the Naples archaeological museum, supported a pergola. There is also an ample quarter with several rooms probably used as *hospitalia*.
The so-called Villa of Cicero, directly opposite the Villa of the Mosaic

Columns, has the same orientation as the Villa of Diomedes, and was also intersected by the road, to which it must have lost many of its rooms. It was brought to light in 1763 and then covered up again. Judging from the Bourbon plan, it was a luxury residence as well as a farm, being equipped with panoramic galleries, porticoes and several stately living rooms. The most important objects found here were two mosaic pictures signed by Dioskourides of Samos, one representing the consulting of a sorceress, a scene drawn from the Middle or New Comedy, the other a group of itinerant musicians. These very fine mosaics derive from paintings of the 3rd century B.C. The original *chiaroscuro* is rendered by using extremely small tesserae.
[L.F.]

26. Column with mosaic decoration, from the Villa of the Mosaic Columns.
Naples, Museo Archeologico Nazionale

⑫ The town walls

(from Porta Ercolano to the Tower of Mercury, No. XI)
Dates of excavation: 1786-1788, 1811, 1812-1813

Since its beginnings in the middle of the 6th century B.C., Pompeii was surrounded by a fortification, as stratigraphic diggings done on several occasions at different points of the walls have shown. Few traces have been found of the most ancient fortification. The only visible remains are outside Porta Nocera. It consisted of a relatively low wall made of blocks of soft lava. At the beginning of the 5th century B.C. it was replaced by a double curtain enclosure made of large limestone slabs, filled in with a conglomerate of earth and rock, a technique of Greek origin which is well visible outside Porta Vesuvio. At the end of the 4th century B.C., at the time of the wars between the Romans and the Samnites, the Greek-type walls were replaced by new ramparts of a type commonly found among Italic populations (Pompeii had been a Samnite city since the end of the 5th century B.C.).

They consisted of a high wall made of large limestone blocks, buttressed on the internal side by an earthwork delimited by a low retaining wall. This is called the "first Samnite phase" of the walls. About a century later, presumably at the time of the Hannibalic war, the ramparts were reinforced, without changing their structure, but using gray tuff this time. The external curtain was raised, an intermediate wall was erected upon the earthwork to create a walkway for the patrolling of the walls, and the earthwork itself was extended inwards, towards the city, and buttressed with a new retaining wall. In some stretches, a tuff staircase (one is well visible near Porta Ercolano) was built against the earthwork to provide easier access to the walkway. The last modification was carried out around the end of the 2nd or beginning of the 1st century B.C., presumably in preparation for the war between Rome and the Italic cities. Long stretches of the outer curtain were reconstructed with the new technique of *opus caementicium* (a conglomerate of stones and mortar),

and astride the walls thirteen towers were built, with an entrance from the city side, exits onto the patrol walkway and posterns on the external side. In the stretch of walls included in this itinerary, i.e. the one between Porta Ercolano and Porta Vesuvio, the two last phases are well represented. On the tuff blocks of the outside curtain, near Porta Ercolano, one can still see the traces of the stone projectiles hurled against the city during its siege by the troops of the Roman general Sulla, who conquered Pompeii in 89 B.C.
[A. d'A.]

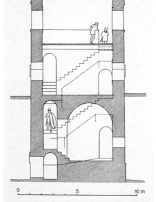

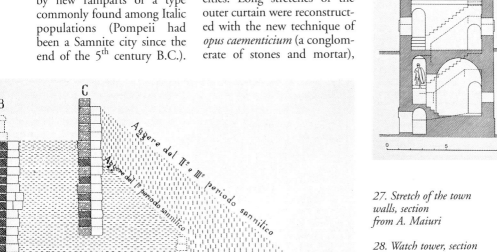

27. Stretch of the town walls, section from A. Maiuri

28. Watch tower, section from E. La Rocca, M. de Vos

29. Official report on the first discoveries at Pompeii in 1748

Poliorcetics

While the use of fortifications goes back to very ancient times, for a long time siege techniques remained underdeveloped. For example, the battering ram only appeared in the second half of the 5th century B.C. It consisted of a large log with a metal point, hanging from a wooden frame on wheels for rapid transportation. A pendulum motion was imparted to the log to send it crashing violently against walls or doors. The name derives from the ram-head shape often given to the metal point. Almost a century later, throwing machines were perfected and became widely diffused. They soon became so powerful as to be able to launch 200 kilo projectiles. The most effective ones were those called by the Romans *tormenta*, which looked somewhat like an oversized crossbow. The impetus was provided by the sudden release of twisted strands of vegetable fibers (*tormenta* comes from *torqueo*, "to twist"). The most common types were the *catapulta*, used to throw large darts, and the *ballista*, which hurled stones. It is presumably *ballistae* that left the marks still visible on the walls of Pompeii near Porta Ercolano, during Sulla's siege of the city in the course of the Social War.

After attacking with these machines, the besiegers sought to reach the summit of the walls by building sloping earthworks on which the soldiers advanced protecting themselves by drawing their shields together (*testudo*), while the besieged attempted to break through their shields by throwing large rocks or dropping upon them lead bars tied with cords to allow them to be drawn back up. Another common siege machine was the *turris ambulatoria*, perfected during the 4th century B.C. They were actual wooden towers with several, progressively narrower stories, high enough to reach the summit of the walls. They rolled on wheels and could be drawn by men or oxen. In the lower story there was a battering ram, in the upper ones throwing machines and movable bridges (*sambucae*) to attack the walls. There were also water reservoirs to put out the flames when the besieged set fire to the tower.

At any rate, the system that Philon of Byzantium (a 2nd century B.C. writer of military treatises) most strongly recommends to besiegers is... to corrupt the generals of the enemy!

[A. d'A.]

CAVA DE LA CIVITA

1748

23 Marzo — Con el motivo de haver estado en los dias pasados al reconocimiento del rio que conduze el agua à la Polvarera en la Torre de la Anunciada, y noticias que tenia precedentemente en particular del Intendente D. Juan Bernardo Boschi, de haver alli un paraje llamado *la civita*, como 2 millas distante de la dicha Torre, donde se han hallado de particular algunas estatuas y otros residuos de la antigua ciudad *Estabia*: me pareciò reconocer el paraje y tomar algunos informes, y he venido à creer que puedan alli encontrarse algunos monumentos y alajas antiguas con menos travajo, que se consigue en este paraje: y con el motivo que haze ya algun tiempo, que en las presentes escavaciones no se halla cosa particular, no obstante que siempre se continuan por entre fabricas arruynadas: yo desearia sumamente suspender aqui por un poco el travajo, é ir à hazer una prueba con la misma gente en el expresado paraje de la civita, y tambien en Gragnano, que es otro lugar no muy distante: en el supuesto de no haumentar en nada el gasto que se haze en la presente escavacion, antes se disminuyria, considerando no ser necesario llevar los forzados en el principio, y hasta ver lo que resulta de las pruevas citadas, pareciendome que siendo la disposicion el que se continue à escavar, es muy conveniente el examinar los citados parajes: à fin de mantener el travajo despues en aquel, que la experiencia haga ver ser el mas abundante. Y si S. M. aprovasse el que se haga esta prueva en ellos, lo que yo deseo mucho, seria necesaria una orden de V. E. para el Govern. de la Torre de la Anunciada, para que facilite el que se pueda establezer el travajo, y el que pueda dormir la gente en algunas casas ò tavernas que hay alli vecino.

27 Marzo — Haviendome dicho S. M. esta mañana que V. E. le havia informado sobre la representacion que hize à

TOM. I.   1

⑬ Crossroads of Orpheus
Date of excavation:
March 31st, 1748

It was here that the first soundings on the plateau "of Civita", near Torre Annunziata, were carried out, after occasional finds during agricultural works were reported. According to the theories circulating at the time, this was the site of ancient Stabiae, although some isolated voices did claim that the ruins that were emerging were those of Pompeii. The latter hypothesis did not find a definitive confirmation until August 16th, 1763, when, near Porta Ercolano, one discovered a cippus with an inscription mentioning the *res publica Pompeianorum*. This is the official report on the first finds, written in Spanish a few days after the beginning of the soundings.

"April 6th [1748]. In the excavation begun at Torre de la Anunciada the most important piece found was a painting 11 palms wide and 4 and a half high (2.904 by 1.188 meters), depicting two great festoons of fruit and flowers, a very large and well-made male head, a helmet, an owl, several birds, and other things; and it seems to me it is one of the best paintings found up to now; and the sculptor, who came with me this morning to see them, has decided to cut them out next Tuesday, as he immediately informed H.M. this evening [...]"

[F. P.]

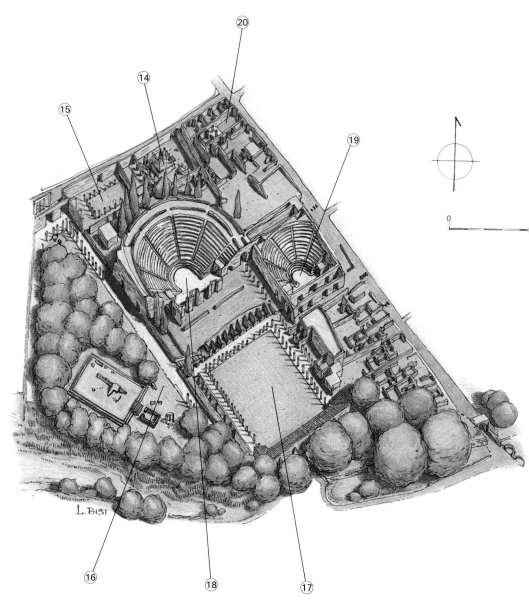

L. BISI

This itinerary comprises the Temple of Isis (14), the Samnite Gymnasium (15), the Triangular Forum (16), the complex of the theaters (17), (18), (19), the Temple of Jupiter Meilichios (20)

The Triangular Forum ⑯ lies on a lava spur from which one dominated the valley and the mouth of the Sarno river. Thanks to this panoramic position, the spur was chosen as the site of one of the most ancient temples of the cities, the Greek-type Doric Temple dedicated to Minerva, built in the 6th century B.C. During the 2nd century B.C., the Triangular Forum and the adjoining area were extensively renovated, becoming a sector of the city devoted to educational and cultural activities. The new buildings included great porticoes around the ancient temple, the Samnite Gymnasium ⑮, the Theater (first phase) ⑱ and the great four-portico courtyard behind it ⑰. In the same period two small temples were erected, probably by private initiative. They were respectively dedicated to Isis ⑭ and Aesculapius ⑳. In the first years of the colony (around 80 B.C.) and in Augustan times, all these buildings were redecorated, but their architecture was left essentially unmodified.
[F.P.]

30. J.W. Huber,
View of the Temple
of Isis, 1820-1837

⑭ Temple of Isis
VIII, 7, 27-28
Dates of excavation:
1764-1766

This sanctuary is enclosed by walls on its north and east sides, the north wall being originally painted with a high red socle and white squares imitating marble blocks, while the east wall was simply coated with rough plaster. It adjoins the Samnite Gymnasium to the west, and the Theater to the south.

As the inscription originally inserted above the entrance tells us, the complex had been damaged by the earthquake of 62 A.D. and entirely rebuilt at his own expense by Numerius Popidius Celsinus, a six-year-old child who was admitted into the collegium decurionum as a reward for this generous deed (actually performed by his father, of course).

Some elements of the tuff architectural decoration, most of which were subsequently covered up with stucco, attest that the earlier building dated from the 2nd century B.C.

The temple was located on December 1764 and brought to light under the careful supervision of Francesco La Vega, who personally undertook the survey of the architecture, while the best draftsmen of the time were called to copy the wall frescoes.

As the rediscovery of Egypt had not yet taken place, the finding of this small sanctuary made a sensation. The Temple of Isis became a must for the many foreigners making the Grand Tour. Many intriguing reconstructive drawings were executed, notably those of Piranesi and Desprez.

The actual temple stands on a high podium with a lava and tuff staircase. It had a pronaos with four Corinthian columns. The inside of the cella was decorated with rectangular squares of white stucco; against its back wall is a bench supporting the tuff bases of the cult statues of Isis and Osiris. The bench is hollow, as it was used as a repository for cult instruments. Another door opens in the south wall of the cella, possibly to allow the priests to enter unseen during the ceremonies. Alongside the main door are two niches for the statues of Harpocrates and Anubis, to which the altars standing at the sides of the podium were dedicated. On the external wall there is a niche where a statue of Dionysus was found, dedicated to Numerius Popidius Ampliatus, the father of Celsinus. The roof was decorated with earthenware slabs bearing bas-reliefs of winged geniuses emerging from trellises and holding cuirasses and shields.

The façade of the *cella* bore a lavish stucco decoration featuring Corinthian pilasters supporting small pediments framing the niches, and stylized architecture graced with wreaths alongside the door. The side and back walls imitated a squared stone wall with Corinthian pilasters at the corners, closed above by a spiral frieze similar to the one painted inside the portico.

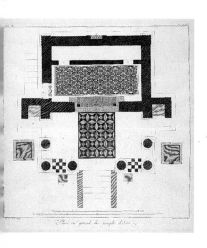

31. G.B. Piranesi,
*The mosaic pavements
of the Temple of Isis*

32. Statue of Isis.
Naples, Museo
Archeologico Nazionale

The niche for the statue of Dionysus at the center of the back wall was decorated with a laurel wreath and flanked by two great ears, also of stucco in relief, symbolizing the goddess' readiness to hear the pleas of the faithful.

The great central courtyard was surrounded by a four-sided portico. At the center of the east side was a pediment above a square niche containing a picture of Harpocrates. In the south side there were entrances to the rooms adjoining the sanctuary (kitchen, cubiculum, triclinium and a space behind the stands of theater). From the west side one entered the *Sacrarium* and the *Ekklesiasterion.* In the northern side of the portico are the entrance to the sanctuary and a small niche decorated with painted emblems of Diana. The pavement of the portico was of simple *cocciopesto*, while in the first building phase there had been a tuff pavement, traces of which can be seen in the trough at the base of the colonnade.

In the portico, altars, bases for votive gifts, marble statues of Isis and Venus, and a bronze portrait of Norbanus Sorex were found. In the north-west corner was a lead pipe with a bronze tap. All these objects are held at the Naples archaeological museum. The four sides of the portico were uniformly decorated with a sequence of red panels framed by golden candelabra or plant stalks connected by wreaths and separated by foreshortened views of buildings. The socle was decorated with yellow panels and partitions. The upper zone of the walls was graced by aedicules connected by carpet edges, wreaths and decorative bands, on a white

background. The middle and upper zones were at once separated and connected horizontally by a long continuous frieze representing an ornate vegetable trellis on a black background, winding its way along the wall in spires amidst half-open flowers, exotic animals and pigmies.

At the center of each of the red panels of the middle zone were represented, alternately, a priest or attendant of the Isiac cult, and a landscape. On the partitions closing off the architectural perspectives were pictures of landscapes, still lifes and naumachiae. Pictures of landscapes and still lifes graced the upper, white background zone as well. At the center of the east wall is a rectangular niche originally containing a painting representing a statue of Harpocrates and a priest advancing towards it with a candelabrum in his hands. The painting was visible from the *cella* of the temple.

In the south corner of the courtyard is an open enclosure delimiting and protecting a staircase leading down into an underground vaulted room with a basin for lustral water whose purifying function gave the small structure its name of *Purgatorium.* It is shaped as an aedicule with a temple façade and an arched entrance toward the north. The walls, topped by female-face antefixes, are entirely coated with stucco.

The façade was decorated with aedicules graced by wreaths and spread veils with dolphins, under which were statues of priestesses of Isis standing on shelves and framed by pilasters adorned by candelabra or acanthus spires enclosing decorative and symbolic figures

(Eros, a bukranion, a uraeus, a scarab, a wheat stalk crown, a hippopotamus, Bes, a sistrum, a situla). The lintel of the pediment featured a procession of offerers and priests in Isiac costumes (including one wearing the Anubis mask) on a blue background. The long side-walls were bordered at the corners by pilasters with candelabra, surmounted by capitals with figures of Harpocrates and Eros, supporting a lintel decorated with amorini and dolphins. On the walls were painted three spread carpets with amorini in flight, Perseus and Andromeda, and Ares and Aphrodite.

West of the courtyard is a great hall with five arched entrances. It is a step higher than the courtyard, and was possibly annexed to the sanctuary in Flavian times, when the latter was renovated by Popidius Celsinus. It has been identified as a *Telesterion* for the performing of sacred dramas, an "Isiac curia" for the holding of ritual banquets, and a *schola* or *Ekklesiasterion* where the meeting of the Isiacs were held. Here were found the marble remains of an acrolithic statue (body of wood, head and limbs of marble) of Isis, possibly the cult image. The goddess is also evoked by the painted candelabra supporting priestesses of Isis gracing the pillars, the details of the socle, and the cult instruments depicted in the great painted scenographies (a golden hydria decorated with gems, a rose crown, and the jug for the lustral water). The paintings of the *Ekklesiasterion* represented a theater scenography with monumental columned wings, large windows opening onto landscapes of Upper and Lower

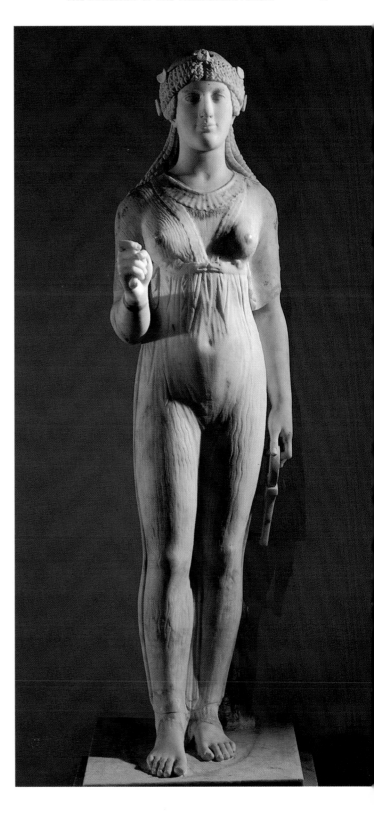

Egypt, and pictures showing scenes of the myth of Io and her arrival to Egypt. The last, framed by red panels, were preserved only on the north and south walls, while the central picture of the west wall was missing. On a lateral avant-corps of the socle were painted sea monsters on a black background, while on the central sector was the Isiac hydria between sphinxes. A landscape, one of the largest frescoes in the collection of the Naples museum, was detached from the west wall together with the decorative elements framing it. It is thus possible to reconstruct the colors of the scenography gracing the wall, which is fully reproduced in an etching by Cataneo.

Five archways leading from the portico to the *Ekklesiasterion* opened in the east wall, which was decorated with a frontal perspective of a portico (presently completely lost) with grooved Corinthian columns on a green background, supporting a red background epistyle with Nereids on dolphins.

The inside of the jambs of the archways was decorated with golden candelabra supporting

statues of Isiac priestesses, each with a different emblem in her hand, painted on a white background. The pavement was of *cocciopesto*, and bore an inscription of white *tesserae* with the names of the donator and his parents: Numerius Popidius Ampliatus, Numerius Popidius Celsinus and Corelia Celsa.

Another room was obtained by annexing part of the area of the Samnite Gymnasium and part of the space behind the external curve of the Theater. It was called *Sacrarium*, and was probably used for the education of new devotees and the preparation of religious ceremonies. It was also a storeroom for the decor of the temple, numerous elements of which were found here.

The painted decoration of this room, probably executed by lararium painters, was the only one in the sanctuary to have a prevalently religious and symbolical character, possibly connected to the instruction of the catechumens who gathered here. The figures were painted in dark colors with broad, diluted brush strokes on a uniform, white background. They include the animals signifying the gods of the

ancient Pharaonic religion (which always appear in the chamber where the cult of the goddess was celebrated), Isis and Osiris enthroned, and the *Navigium Isidis*, one of the main events in Isiac religion, i.e. Isis transporting the body of Osiris along the Nile towards a new life, after having found and recomposed it. The groups and scenes were not framed by architectural structures or partitioned by decorative elements, and there was no landscape in the background. On entering, the faithful was confronted with the two gods sitting on the throne between a lion, a cobra and a scarab. Further to the right was Bes and, beyond the masonry shrine, the transportation of the body of Osiris along the Nile by the maternal and life-giving Isis, with a cobra and a vulture attending the scene. A lion and an ibis faced a group of animals on the east wall, comprising a baboon, a ram, a jackal, a mouse, a vulture and a mongoose. At the southern extremity of the same wall, a bull was depicted.

From the south side of the portico one entered a group of secondary rooms, presumably the *pastophorion* where the priests lived. A cubiculum, a triclinium and a kitchen have been recognized, while the function of the irregular room along the curved wall of the theater is unknown. Fragments of an earthenware well curb, possibly from a reservoir lying north of the *Purgatori-*

33. G. Chiantarelli, Fresco on the south wall of the Ekklesiasterion of the Temple of Isis, 1810

um, were found in the cubiculum or the triclinium. These two rooms were also graced by Fourth Style paintings, typical of the last decades of the life of the city.

The frescoes of the sanctuary belong to two distinctive genres: the Fourth Style of the portico, *Ekklesiasterion*, cubiculum and triclinium, and the "popular" or "lararium" style of the paintings in the *Sacrarium*.

The sacred character of the temple is alluded to only by the figures of priests, priestesses and attendants, mostly dressed in white and holding the objects used in the cult of the goddess, mainly known from their description by Lucius Apuleius in his novel *Metamorphoses*. References to Egypt can be found in the landscapes, in the animals populating the spiralling frieze, and in decorative figures such as the sphinxes, lionesses, crocodiles, cobra and mongoose. The subjects of the mythological pictures in the *Ekklesiasterion* appear in houses in Rome, Pompeii and Herculaneum. Representations of Io between Argos and Hermes are especially common, while the arrival of Io in Canopus is known from only one other replica found in a Pompeian house. In general, it can be said that the pictorial decoration of the sanctuary does not have an explicitly religious character.

[V.S.]

The cult of Isis

The temple was dedicated to Isis, an Egyptian deity whose cult had been introduced in Italy, especially in the Greek colonies in Sicily, as early as the 4th century B.C. In the 2nd century there were already temples dedicated to her in towns which had commercial relationships with Egypt. In Rome there was a long-lasting resistance to the introduction of an official cult of Isis, although ceremonies in her honor are reported as early as the 1st century B.C. It was only under Caligula that her great temple on the Campo Marzio was built.

In her Greek-Roman cult, Isis was identified with almost all the main goddesses: Demeter, Aphrodite, Hecate, Semele, Artemis, Nemesis, Hera, Tyche etc. Being called "Isis of the endless names", she was regarded as the giver of life and queen of the elements. The great popularity, initially only in private domains, of the cult of the goddess and her spouse Osiris (Serapis in the Greek version), was due to the redemptory and miraculous character of her cult, which promised life and happiness after death. One of the most important feasts of the cult of Isis was the *Navigium Isidis*, re-evoking the transportation along the Nile of the cadaver of Osiris, reassembled after the evil Typhon had killed the god, dismembered his body and dispersed its pieces. The feast was celebrated at the beginning of March, with the return of spring and the resuming of navigation. Another feast at the beginning of November re-evoked the death of Osiris, the search for his body and his resurrection by the agency of Isis' magical powers. All the ceremonies in honor of the goddess were public. Her statue was adored every morning, after receiving a series of offerings and libations in which Nile water played an important role. The only ceremony that took place behind closed doors was the initiation of priests, a vivid description of which is provided by Lucius Apuleius in his novel *Metamorphoses*.

[V.S.]

⑮ Samnite Gymnasium (Isiac Curia; building called "triibús"; Gymnasium of Vinicius)

VIII, 7, 29
Dates of excavation:
1768, 1796-1798

An Oscan inscription dated to the 2nd century B.C., re-employed after the earthquake of 62 A.D. in the wall separating the Gymnasium from the Temple of Isis, informs us that the building was built by a magistrate of the city with money that Vibius Adiranus had willed to the *vereia* of Pompeii, an aristocratic political and military association also attested in other Samnite towns of ancient Italy. Both

entered a courtyard with porticoes on three sides. The only rooms lay behind the west portico, right of the entrance. They probably comprised dressing rooms (*apodyteria*) and a room where the athlets cleansed themselves (*destrictarium*). The asymmetrical structure of the building, which lacks a fourth portico on the east side, is the result of post-earthquake renovation, when part of this side was incorporated by the adjacent Temple of Isis and a new dividing wall was built over the old trough. Most of the original tuff Doric columns of the porticoes to the right and in front of the entrance (west and south) are still preserved.

This deity was probably Hermes, the protector of youth and athletes, whose image was presumably of bronze. The statue of the Doriphorus, found nearby, could not possibly have stood on the base, as the form and size of the statue's plinth do not fit the cavity on top of the base itself. A close study of the three tuff structures has established that their present-day arrangement is not the original one. At the time of the construction of the gymnasium only the statue base was there, and it was used as an altar. Later on, in early Imperial times, the altar was converted into a statue base, and the altar and staircase were added. The tuff structures also show signs of post-earthquake restoration, as the statue base has a large stone nog on the side towards the staircase, and the upper block of the altar was carved out of one of the tuff steps of the *Odeion*.
[F.P.]

the structure and the position of the building identify it as a gymnasium, since it is near the racing track in the Triangular Forum and an old thermal plant on the corner between Via dei Teatri and Via del Tempio di Iside (VIII, 5, 36), which a modern plaque labels "Republican Thermae". A secondary entrance opened directly onto the covered racing track under the east portico of the Triangular Forum. From the main entrance on Via del Tempio di Iside one

They were surmounted by a Doric frieze with triglyphs, a few fragments of which are still visible between the columns of the west portico. On the axis of the entrance, in front of the south portico, one behind the other, are an altar, a high statue base and a staircase, all made of tuff. During the ceremonies that took place in the gymnasium, the statue on the base was crowned and offerings to the deity adored by the athletes were placed upon the altar.

34. Oscan epigraph from the Samnite Gymnasium. Naples, Museo Archeologico Nazionale

35. Statue of the Doriphorus from the Samnite Gymnasium. Naples, Museo Archeologico Nazionale

The Doriphorus of the Samnite Gymnasium

From the Augustan age onward, many buildings of the Triangular Forum were restructured. The most radical renovation was carried out in the Large Theater and the nearby *Odeion*, whose floors and walls were faced with marble. In the same period, some more limited, but nevertheless remarkable works were undertaken in the area: a semicircular seat and a meridian were dedicated near the Doric Temple, a fountain basin and a statue of Marcellus were installed in front of the portico of the entrance in the Triangular Forum, and the Samnite Gymnasium was redecorated. In the last, in early Imperial times, the ancient tuff altar was transformed into a monumental base, and a great marble statue was dedicated. This sculpture, 2 meters tall, was found broken in several pieces in the south portico sometime between April 15th and August 19th, 1797. It is one of the most complete copies of the Doriphorus ("lance-bearer") of Polycletus, whose bronze original, made about 440 B.C., was the most lofty and celebrated work of the great sculptor of Argos. The statue was a sculptural synthesis of the principles of harmony of form theorized by Polycletus in a treatise called Κανών (*Canon*, a name ancient writers sometimes used for the statue itself. Aside from the perfect proportioning of the body, the most remarkable quality of Polycletus' masterpiece lies in the discovery of an ideal formal system to give the beholder the impression of a body in motion, concluding a quest which had absorbed two generations of Greek sculptors, from

Kritios and Nesiotes (ca. 480 B.C.) to Myron (450 B.C.). The impression of movement results from the double convergence of imaginary lines following the profile of the shoulders and the pelvis, and that of the shins. This pattern is echoed by the opposition between tense limbs (the right leg, carrying the weight of the body, and the left arm, holding the spear) and relaxed ones (the left leg, flexed backwards, but ready to advance, and the right arm at rest alongside the body). The Doriphorus represents an armed young man, possibly Achilles, a fit subject to celebrate both military life and sports, which were always closely related in the value system of the ruling classes of Greek or Hellenized communities. Thus, the statue is well suited for the seat of this ancient Samnite military institution, the *vereia*, architecturally structured as a gymnasium, and reveals a will to integrate even the most ancient public buildings into the process of monumental renovation of the public areas of Pompeii during the Augustan age. This redecoration of the Samnite Gymnasium was possibly undertaken by Marcus Lucretius Decidianus Rufus, one of the most influential Pompeian aristocrats of the first decades of the 1st century B.C., as the excavation diary mentions the discovery, on August 19th, 1797, of an inscription commemorating Rufus' brilliant political and military career, and mentioning his sponsoring the construction of buildings which were restored, after the earthquake of 62 A.D., by Marcus Decidius Pilonius *(M. Lucretius Decid./ Rufus IIvir III quinq./ pontif. trib.*

mil. a populo/ praef. fabr./ M. Decidius Pilonius/ Rufus reposuit). The incorporation of the east side of the building into the adjacent temple of Isis, and the repairs still visible of the tuff bases of the south side of the portico, presumably go back to this restoration. [F.P.]

⑯ Triangular Forum

VIII, 7, 30-34
Dates of excavation:
1765, 1767-1768, 1773,
1796-1797, 1813

The entrance to the Triangular Forum, lying near a crossroads, is fronted by a monumental propylon originally comprising six tuff Ionic columns, bordered by pillars graced by semi-columns of the same type. After the excavation, three columns and one semi-column were restored. A fragment of the great architrave they supported is still preserved. The propylon goes back to the 2nd century B.C., but its back wall, in which two doorways open, was completely rebuilt in *opus incertum* and *opus latericium* after the earthquake of 62 A.D. From the left door, one enters the great three-sided portico delimiting

the sacred area, supported by about 100 tuff columns, only a few of which were found intact. Eleven columns have been restored in the long east portico. They are surmounted by a Doric frieze, and look very much like those of the nearby Samnite Gymnasium. Near the entrance are a fountain basin and a marble-faced base for a statue of Marcellus (Augustus' nephew), honored in the inscription as *patronus*. It has been suggested that the entire eastern portico and the side of the square delimited by a long and low wall beginning immediately behind the statue of Marcellus were used respectively as a covered race-track (*xystus*) and an open-air one. This hypothesis is quite plausible, considering that this area was connected to the Samnite Gymnasium by a secondary entrance. If this area was truly

used as a gymnasium, it would have been placed under the protection of one of the most ancient cult buildings of the city, as the Triangular Forum was the seat of the Doric Temple, which dates back to the middle of the 6th century B.C. A series of finds has shown that this temple was redecorated several times between the 5th and the 2nd century B.C. Its original plan is not very clear, as the building was already in a state of abandonment at the time of the eruption of 79 A.D. However, it is certain that it was completely surrounded by columns, an architectural feature typical of Greek temples, and that it faced the terrace. Four of the original Doric capitals, made of Sarno limestone, have been arranged at its corners. The temple was almost certainly dedicated to Minerva, as an Oscan inscription read in Via dell'Abbondanza, shortly before its intersection with Via dei Teatri, refers to the presence in this area of a temple of this goddess. Around the temple there are other monuments as well. Almost adjoining its north-west corner is a semicircular tuff seat whose extremities are graced by winged lion paws. Its Latin inscription, of the Augustan age, informs us that the seat, called a *"schola"*, was dedicated, along with a meridian, by the duoviri Lucius Sepunius Sandilianus and Marcus Herennius Epidianus. Three small tuff bases, identifiable as altars, lie in front of the temple, left of a rectangu-

*36. View of the
Triangular Forum
and the exterior
of the Large Theater*

lar enclosure whose presently visible remains date from the Augustan age. It was almost certainly the symbolic tomb (*heroon*) of the mythical founder of the city. Behind the enclosure is a well surrounded by a round shrine (*tholos*), of which four tuff Doric columns remain. An Oscan inscription on the architrave announced that this elegant construction was the work of the supreme magistrate of the city, the *(meddix)* Numerius Trebius. The function of this well is doubtful. It has been observed that its curb shows no sign of wear due to rope friction. Being near the tomb of the founder of the city, the shrine was possibly a *mundus*, like the one in the Forum of Rome, i.e. the meeting place of the world of the living with the netherworld, which was closely connected to the elaborate rites preceding the foundation of cities.
[F.P.]

37. C. Weichardt,
*Ideal reconstruction
of the Greek Temple
and the tholos in the
Triangular Forum, 1897*

38. Anonymous,
*Reconstruction
of the tholos in the
Triangular Forum,
early 19th century*

⑰ *Porticus post scaenam* (Quartiers des Soldats; The Gladiators' Barracks)

VIII, 7, 16-17
Dates of excavation:
1766-1769, 1771,
1792-1795

A flight of stairs connects the Triangular Forum to the large four-sided portico behind the Large Theater, surrounded by 74 columns of stuccoed tuff, many of which were restored in modern times. The building, dating from the 2nd century B.C., was originally a *porticus post scaenam*, i.e. a great porticoed space used by the spectators during the in-tervals of the shows, and to seek shelter in case of rain. The building of such porti-coes is recommended by the Roman architect Vitruvius. Sometimes they enclosed highly ornate gardens, like in the huge Porticoes of Pompey in Rome, built in 55 B.C., an appropriate background for a valuable collection of statues and paintings by famous Greek artists. Originally, the only room of the Pompeian *porticus post scaenam* was the great exedra at the center of the south side. All the other rooms go back to a renovation following the earthquake of 62 A.D., when the building was converted into gladiator barracks (*ludus*). The accesses to the theater were walled up, the final stretch of the great staircase was partially disman-tled, and the great exedra was decorated with paintings de-picting Mars and Venus, and trophies of gladiator weapons. The most important rooms were built along the east side of the portico. The great exe-dra, fronted by four brick-work pillars, was the refectory, while the rooms on the upper floor presumably were the quarters of the gladiator con-tractor (the *lanista*). In this group of rooms, in two wood-en boxes, were found some

cloths embroidered with golden threads and numerous lavishly ornamented weapons used by the gladiators for the parades preceding the games. The eruption of the Vesuvius took a heavy toll here. Four skeletons were found near a beam fitted with clogs in a room opening onto the west side of the portico, obviously a jail. In another room were the remains of 18 people, including a woman adorned with magnificent jewellery. [F.P.]

39. A. Vianelli,
"Quadriportico"
of the soldiers
(or of the Theater), 1837

40. G.B. Piranesi,
Prisoners in the
Gladiator Barracks.
Berlin, Staatliche Museen,
Kupferstichkabinett

41. Parade gladiator
weapons.
Naples, Museo
Archeologico Nazionale

⑱ Large Theater (Tragic Theater)

VIII, 7, 20-21; 27 and 30
Dates of excavation:
1764-1765, 1767-1769,
1773, 1789, 1791, 1794

The present appearance of the Large Theater is essentially the result of the renovations of the Augustan period, although there are still traces of the preceding phases, on one hand, and of the restorations following the earthquake of 62 A.D. on the other. The theater was built around the middle of the 2nd century B.C., and hence is coeval with the theaters of the Campanian cities of Teano, Cales and Capua. It was built of *opus incertum* and rested against the natural slope of the hill. Excavation has revealed that, in its first phase, the *cavea*, made of tuff or limestone steps, was delimited at its extremities by retaining walls facing the original *parodoi* (passages leading into the orchestra) which, like those of Greek theaters, were open. At a later date, probably during the first years of the colonial period (ca. 80-70 B.C.), the *parodoi* were roofed in, and the *cavea* was extended over them. Renovation works undertaken in the Augustan period by the architect Marcus Artorius Primus, a former slave (his name is mentioned in an inscription on the wall near the east entrance to the orchestra, presently in the Naples archaeological museum, and replaced by a copy), were certainly sponsored by two members of one of the most eminent families of the city, whose wealth was founded on the production and sale of wine, viz. Marcus Holconius Rufus and Marcus Holconius Celer. An inscription in three copies, two whole and one fragmentary, kept in the Naples museum, recalls that the two *Holconii* brothers sponsored, at their own expense (*sua pecunia*), the construction of the covered passage (*cryptam*), the stage boxes (*tribunalia*) for honorary guests replacing the steps overlying the vaults of the *parodoi*, and all the steps (*theatrum*). Their munificence was rewarded with the erection of honorary statues in the theatre. Holconius Rufus was also honored with a *bisellium*, the seat normally reserved to the decurions. It was located at the exact midpoint of the lower step of the *media cavea*, from where one had the best view of the stage, and was marked by an inscription in bronze letters of which only the slots in the travertine steps remain. The *cavea*, crowned by an annular barrel-vaulted passage (the *crypta* of the inscription of the *Holconii*), was

divided by annular passageways into three zones, the *ima, media* and *summa cavea* (from bottom to top), in their turn subdivided into five sections by six vertical passageways (*kerkides*). The *ima cavea*, reserved to the members of the local Senate, comprised four rows of seats. The *media cavea* had twenty rows, and the *summa cavea*, very little of which is preserved, probably only four. The two upper zones were reached through entrances opening at the level of the Triangular Forum. Between the *ima cavea* and the stage is the orchestra, horseshoe-shaped, onto which open the two covered *parodoi*, which communicate with a courtyard lying behind the scene. The east *parodos* leads to the Via Stabiana, the west one to the Triangular Forum. The keystone of the arch of the latter is graced by a Nocera tuff satyr head which, like the vault itself, dates back to the Sullan period. The low front of the stage (*proskenion*) is partitioned by niches and steps used by the actors to climb and descend from the stage. The narrow groove with cavities for beams behind the front of the *proskenion* was used to contain the curtain, which was drawn up from below at the end of the performance or during the intervals. At the back of the stage stands the *frons scaenae*. Its remaining vestiges date from its reconstruction after the earthquake of 62 A.D., when it was probably raised to two stories reproducing the façade of a princely palace. It had three doorways – one in the central apse, the others on the sides – leading to a backstage room communicating with the courtyard, possibly used as a dressing room.

[F. P.]

42. F. Mazois,
View of the Large Theater
(Mazois, IV, pl. XXX)

43. J.-L. Desprez,
Ideal Reconstruction of the Quarter of the Soldiers and the Quarter of the Theater,
in Saint-Non, *Voyage pittoresque, I, pl. 200*

⑲ *Odeion*
(Small Theater;
Theatrum tectum)
VIII, 7, 17-20
Dates of excavation:
1769, 1792-1795

Inserted in the wall separating the *Odeion* from a small porticoed courtyard connecting the Large Theater to the *porticus post scaenam*, is one of two inscriptions commemorating the construction of the *Odeion* itself (a second, identical one surmounts the entrance from Porta Stabiana). It is incised on a re-employed travertine doorstep, and recites: "Gaius Quinctius Valgus, the son of Gaius, and Marcus Porcius, the son of Marcus, *duoviri*, by will of the decurions, contracted out the building of the roofed theater (*theatrum tectum*), and tested it." These two men, who held the highest municipal office in the first years of the Sullan colony, also had the Amphitheater built in the same period. The walls of the *Odeion*, made of *opus quasi reticulatum*, a masonry core faced with oblique, but still not perfectly aligned rows of square-faced lava stones (hence the name), date from this period, as well as most of its Second Style frescoes, traces of which could still be seen by 19th-century scholars, but completely vanished today. As in the Large Theater, there were several entrances, used to reach the sectors reserved to the different classes, subdivided according to a rigid hierarchy. By the vaulted corridors (*parodoi*) one entered the semicircular orchestra paved with marble slabs. An inscription in bronze letters (only the slots of which were seen by the excavators)

attributed to the duovir Marcus Oculatius Verus, who lived under Augustus, the construction of this pavement, which was financed with the funds for the theater performances. Above the *parodoi* are boxes for the authorities. The decurions' stools were placed on the first four rows of steps, the *ima cavea*, separated from the *media cavea* above by a tuff partition adorned at the extremities by winged lion paws. Behind this partition was a walkway giving access to four narrow staircases dividing the steps into five sectors. At the top, the sides of the *media cavea* are cut short by the thick perimetral walls originally supporting the roof of the building, which must have been dou-

ble-eaved and supported by five trusses. While the stage is very simple, with a channel containing the curtain in front and three doorways leading to the actors' dressing rooms, the *analemmata* are elaborately decorated, being surmounted by a modeled cornice and graced, at their extremities, by sculpted tuff telamones very similar to the stuccoed earthenware ones in the Terme del Foro, and the kneeling Atlases supporting the globe in the Theater of Pietrabbondante in the Pentran Samnium (Molise).

This building is generally regarded as a theater for instrumental and singing performances, roofed in to improve its acoustics. The pairing of such an auditorium with a

larger theater used for the performing of tragedies and comedies is mentioned by the poet Statius for the nearby city of Neapolis. According to two different recent hypotheses, the *Odeion* was originally a public building with a political function, transformed into a roofed theater only from the Augustan age onward. Up to then, it served as a *curia*, i.e. as the seat of the local Senate, according to one hypothesis, or as the meeting-place of the Sullan colonists who settled in Pompeii in 80 B.C., according to the other. However, the capacity of the *Odeion*, which could contain between 1,500 and 2,000 spectators, is enormously superior to the number of the decurions who, even under the Empire, amounted to barely 100. As to the second hypothesis, there is no evidence to confirm it, either in Pompeii, where the Forum was extensively renovated after the establishment of the colony, or elsewhere. In the present state of our knowledge, it is preferable to continue to employ for the building the same expression used by its builders, viz. *theatrum tectum*.

[F.P.]

The epigrams of *Tiburtinus*

On the left wall of the *Odeion*, many graffiti were read in the 19th century, including two neoteric-flavored epigrams signed by a certain *Tiburtinus*, datable between 80 and 70 B.C., i.e. shortly before the flourishing in Rome of celebrated poets such as Catullus, Licinius Calvus, Elvius Cinna and Cornelius Gallus.
"What is going on? Oh eyes, that drew me by force into the fire, do not force tears onto my cheeks. Sure, tears cannot put the flame out. Such things set one's face on fire and wear out the soul. Tiburtinus composed [this]."
"If you know what love can do, if you consider yourself human, have mercy on me, let me come. The flower of Venus to me [...]"
[F.P.]

44. A. Vianelli, Interior of the Small Theater, ca. 1837

⑳ Temple of Jupiter Meilichios (Temple of the Capitoline Triad; Temple of Neptune; Temple of Aesculapius)

VIII, 7, 25
Dates of excavation:
1766, 1798

This small temple, completely surrounded by an *opus incertum* enclosure, comprises an open courtyard from which a staircase leads up to a podium with a *cella* at the back made of *opus quasi reticulatum*. Immediately past the entrance was a small portico; only the foundation of its two columns remains. A room probably used by the ministers of the cult opened onto this portico. At the base of the staircase is an altar faced with tuff slabs, decorated above by a Doric frieze (triglyphs and metopae) surmounted by a jutting cornice and dosserets with Ionic volutes, a style which became popular in the Hellenistic period. Both the structure of the temple and the altar seem datable to the 2nd century B.C., while the masonry of the walls of the cella must date back to the Sullan period. The entrance portico, with its two brick columns, presumably dates back to the restorations following the earthquake of 62 A.D.

An earthenware statue and two busts of the same material, found in the cella, and an Oscan inscription found near Porta di Stabia are the elements on which the controversial identification of the tutelary god of the temple is based. Leaving aside the bust, which undoubtedly depicts Minerva, the two statues were initially identified by Winckelmann as the god of medicine Aesculapius and his daughter Hygeia. Later on, von Rohden interpreted them as Jupiter and Juno; thus, the temple would have been dedicated to the Capitoline Triad. In the meantime, Nissen had identified the building with the temple of Jupiter Meilichios mentioned in the Oscan epigraph. At the end of the 19th century, Mau came to the conclusion that the temple was indeed that of Jupiter Meilichios but, after the severe damage wrought by the earthquake of 62 A.D. to the *Capitolium* in the Forum, the statues of Jupiter, Juno and Minerva had been brought here. This has been the com-

monly accepted interpretation to this day. De Caro, however, has recently observed that the cult of Jupiter Meilichios, being funerary in character, would hardly have been practiced inside the city. Furthermore, some objects found in the room on the right of the portico (especially a bone casket decorated with figures of Apollo as a physician and Hygeia) seem to suggest that the temple was dedicated to salutary deities, viz. Aesculapius and Hygeia, possibly associated with Minerva in her role of *Minerva Medica*. According to De Caro, the actual temple of Jupiter Meilichios must have lain outside the city, and could possibly be identified with a partially explored suburban sanctuary in the "Fondo Iozzino", at a short distance from Pompeii.
[A.d'A.]

*45. A. Vianelli,
Temple of Jupiter
Meilichios,
before 1827-1828*

*46. Earthenware statue
of Aesculapius.
Naples, Museo
Archeologico Nazionale*

The earthenware statues of the Temple of Jupiter Meilichios

Earthenware statues were made by means of moulds, and have flat backs which were hidden to the gaze of the observer, as the figures were placed against walls.

The female statue, wearing a cloak (*himation*) over a long tunic (*chyton*), has an abnormally elongated figure, a stylistic trait typical of Italic art. The pleats of the underlying tunic show through the cloak, a feature harking back to late Hellenistic art, being commonly associated with the sculptor Phyliscus of Rhodes. The pose of the figure, position of the arms and typology of the tunic are similar to those found in statues of the goddess of health, Hygeia, harking back to sculptural models of the Hellenistic period. As to the male figure, the attitude of the body and legs, the coiffure and the cloak are almost identical to those of sculptures representing the god of medicine, Aesculapius. However, when, as in this statue, the rod with the snake wound coiled around it (in this case it would have been held by the right hand), the characteristic attribute of Aesculapius, is lacking, the iconography of this god, created in the 4th century, can be confused with that of contemporary images of Zeus and Poseidon.

The bust, which the helmet, shield and aegis identify as the goddess Minerva, was made with a single mould and completed with appliqués. At the center of the small shield there must have been an appliqué representing a Gorgon head, like the one on the aegis at the center of the breast. If the identification of the two preceding statues as Aesculapius and Hygeia is correct, the bust should represent Minerva Medica.
[A. d'A]

47. Earthenware bust of Minerva Medica. Naples, Museo Archeologico Nazionale

48. Earthenware statue
of Hygeia.
Naples, Museo
Archeologico Nazionale

AMPHITHEATER

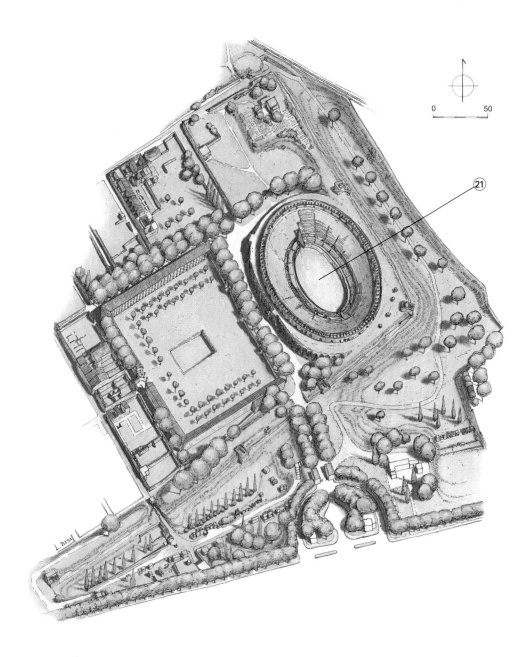

One reaches the
Amphitheater ㉑
by walking along Via
dell'Abbondanza up to
the house of Decimus
Octavius Quartio (II, 2, 2)

㉑ Amphitheater

II, 6
Dates of excavation:
1748, 1813-1816

The amphitheater, lying at the edge of the city, is the most imposing of the Pompeian buildings. It had a capacity of over 20.000 seats enabling it to host spectators from the neighboring cities as well. It leaned against the south-east corner of the walls, and was supported by an earthwork obtained by digging the arena, which lies almost six meters below the ground level outside the amphitheater. The stands were built upon the earthwork, which was retained by a scarped wall with radial bulwarks spanned by blind arches supporting a walkway providing access to the *summa cavea*. Six large external staircases, also supported by arches, led up to this walkway.

The amphitheater, called *spectacula* in the dedicatory inscription affixed by the magistrates who personally financed its construction and donated it to the colony, is the most ancient preserved building of its kind. It dates from the early years of the colony, i.e. the first half of the 1st century B.C. It is a typically Italic architectural invention created by juxtaposing two very elongated theater *caveae* around an oval arena.

Access to the *media* and *ima cavea* was assured by vaulted galleries connected to a covered annular passage from which, through the *vomitoria*, the spectators went up to the stands. The *cavea* was divided into wedges whose stone steps were gradually completed by several magistrates over the years. In the *ima cavea* there were separate boxes for the local notables. There were two doors at each extremity of the long axis of the arena. From the *Porta Triumphalis* the *pompa* came in, i.e. the parade of the participants in the games. From the *Porta Libitinensis* the dead gladiators and animals were brought out. Linen shades were mounted on wooden poles steadied by guy ropes to shield the spectators from the fiery rays of the sun.

[A.V.]

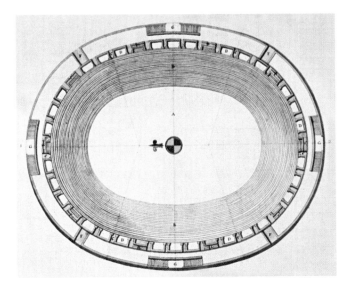

49. K. Weber,
Amphitheater, 1748

Gladiator games

It seems that gladiator games first appeared in Campania. Initially, they were celebrated in honor of the dead, a custom attested by funerary paintings of Oscan-speaking Campanian and Lucanian peoples as early as the 4th century B.C. They were extremely popular in Pompeii, where numerous announcements of shows were found on the walls of many buildings and enthusiastic ovations were given to the *editores munerum*, the sponsors of the games who, through contractors (*lanistae*), hired *familiae gladiatoriae*, i.e. teams of gladiators specializing in one or another of several types of weapons, sometimes recruited and maintained by wealthy private citizens. Other graffiti seem to be reports on a *munus*, recording the results of the matches and the curriculum of the gladiators.

The show generally comprised two parts, viz. combats between gladiators and combats against animals. In Pompeii, the game announcements mention from 10 (reading uncertain) to 49 gladiator pairs, but most often 20, which must have been the standard number. Gladiators were trained in special schools, an especially renowned one being the Imperial school of Capua, formerly belonging to Caesar. Besides stirring the enthusiasm of the public, gladiators also broke many female hearts, as many graffiti bear out. During a gladiator match in 59 A.D., a bloody fight broke out between Pompeians and Nucerians, reproduced with nearly photographic realism in a famous fresco. Following this riot, Nero prohibited the celebrating of games in the amphitheater of Pompeii for ten years. The ban was removed, however, sometime after the earthquake of 62 A.D. [A.V.]

50. F. Morelli, *Amphitheater, friezes with gladiators, before 1816*

51. F. Morelli, *Amphitheater, painted podium with a Victory and frieze with a paradeisos, before 1816*

52. *Fight between Pompeians and Nucerians, fresco from Pompeii. Naples, Museo Archeologico Nazionale*

53. F. Mazois, *Gladiators (Mazois, IV, pl. XI)*

BIBLIOGRAPHY

All the excavation dates referred to in this volume are drawn from H.B. Van der Poel, *Corpus Topographicum Pompeianum V. Cartography*, Rome 1981.

FORUM

1 BASILICA
K. Ohr, *Die Basilica in Pompeji*, Karlsruhe 1973.

VIA CONSOLARE

6 HOUSE OF PANSA
F. Pesando, *"Domus". Edilizia privata e società pompeiana fra III e I secolo a. C.*, Soprintendenza Archeologica di Pompei. Monografie 12, Rome 1997, pp. 68-78.
G.O. Onorato, *Inscriptiones Pompeianae. Honores et munera*, Florence 1957, pp. 54-55.

7 *THERMOPOLIUM* OF FORTUNATA
F. Pesando, in F. Carocci, E. De Albentiis, M. Gargiulo, F. Pesando, *Le insulae 3 e 4 della Regio VI di Pompei*, Rome 1990, pp. 138-141.

8 HOUSE OF THE BAKER
F. Carocci, in F. Carocci, E. De Albentiis, M. Gargiulo, F. Pesando, *Le insulae 3 e 4 della Regio VI di Pompei*, Rome 1990, pp. 19-56.

9 HOUSE OF THE SURGEON
A. Maiuri, in *Notizie degli Scavi* (1930), pp. 380 ff.
Id., *Alla ricerca di Pompei preromana (Saggi stratigrafici)*, Naples 1973, pp. 2 ff.
C. Chiaramonte Treré, "Sull'origine e lo sviluppo dell'architettura residenziale di Pompei sannitica", *Acme* 43 (1990), fasc. 3, pp. 3 ff.

NECROPOLIS OF PORTA ERCOLANO

10 NECROPOLIS OF PORTA ERCOLANO
V. Kockel, *Die Grabbauten vor dem Herkulaner Tor in Pompeji*, Mainz 1983.

11 VILLA OF DIOMEDES
A. Maiuri, R. Pane, *La casa di Loreio Tiburtino e la Villa di Diomede*, Rome 1947.

12 TOWN WALLS
A. Maiuri, "Studi e ricerche sulle fortificazioni di Pompei", *Monumenti Antichi dell'Accademia dei Lincei* 33 (1930), cols. 114-276.
S. De Caro, "Nuove indagini sulle fortificazioni di Pompei", *Annali dell'Istituto Universitario Orientale di Napoli. Sezione di Archeologia e Storia Antica* 7 (1985), pp. 75-114.

TRIANGULAR FORUM

14 TEMPLE OF ISIS
S. De Caro, V. Sampaolo a. o., *Alla ricerca di Iside*, Rome 1992.

15 SAMNITE GYMNASIUM
A. and M. de Vos, *Pompei, Ercolano, Stabia*, Guide Archeologiche Laterza, Rome-Bari 1982, pp. 71-72.
P. Poccetti, "Il testamento di Vibio Adirano", *Rendiconti dell'Accademia di Lettere e Belle Arti di Napoli* 57 (1982), pp. 227-245 (on the Oscan inscription).
E. Pernice, *Die hellenistische Kunst in Pompeji, V. Hellenistische Tische, Zisternenmündungen, Beckenuntersätze, Altäre und Truhen*, Berlin 1932, pp. 58-60 (a study of the tuff structures).
P. Zanker, *Klassizistische Statuen. Studien zur Veränderung des Kunstgeschmacks in der römischen Kaiserzeit*, Mainz 1974, p. 8 (dating of the Doriphorus to the time of Tiberius).
D. Kreikenbom, *Bildwerke nach Polyklet*, Berlin 1990, p. 163 (dating of the Doriphorus late in the reign of Tiberius).

16 TRIANGULAR FORUM
A. et M. de Vos, *Pompei, Ercolano, Stabia*, Guide Archeologiche Laterza, Rome-Bari 1982, pp. 60-64.

J.A.K.E. De Waele, "Excavations in the Doric Temple on the Triangular Forum at Pompeii (15-26 july 1996)", *Opuscula Pompeiana* 7 (1997), pp. 51-73 (report on recent stratigraphic soundings in the Doric Temple).
M. Verzar, "L'umbilicus urbis. Il mundus in età tardo-repubblicana", *Dialoghi di Archeologia* 9-10 (1976-1977), pp. 378-398 (especially pp. 395-396 on the interpretation of the *tholos* as a *mundus*).

17 *PORTICUS POST SCAENAM*
A. and M. de Vos, *Pompei, Ercolano, Stabia*, Guide Archeologiche Laterza, Rome-Bari 1982, pp. 67-69.
P. Zanker, *Pompei. Società, immagini urbane e forme dell'abitare*, Turin 1993, pp. 52-56 (identification of the *porticus post scaenam* as a gymnasium of Samnite Pompeii).

18 LARGE THEATER
A. Maiuri, "Saggi nella cavea del Teatro Grande", *Notizie degli Scavi* (1951), pp. 126-134.
H. Lauter, "Die hellenistischen Theater der Samniten und Latiner in ihrer Beziehung zur Theaterarchitektur der Griechen", in P. Zanker (ed.), *Hellenismus in Mittelitalien*, Acts of the meeting held in Göttingen from 5th to 9th June 1974, Göttingen 1976, pp. 415-418.

19 *ODEION*
M. Murolo, "Il cosidetto 'Odeo' di Pompei e il problema della sua copertura", *Rendiconti dell'Accademia di Archeologia, Lettere e Belle Arti di Napoli*, n. s. 34 (1959), pp. 89-101.
J.-Ch. Balty, *Curia Ordinis. Recherches d'architecture et d'urbanisme antiques sur les curies provinciales du monde romain*, Brussels 1991, pp. 593-595 (the *Odeion* used as a *curia*).
P. Zanker, *Pompei. Società,*

*immagini urbane e forme
dell'abitare*, Turin 1993,
pp. 74-77 (the *Odeion* used
as a meeting place for Sullan
colonists).
M. Gigante, *Civiltà delle forme
letterarie nell'antica Pompei*,
Naples 1979 (on the poems
of Tiburtinus).

**20 TEMPLE OF JUPITER
MEILICHIOS**
D. Russo, *Il Tempio di Giove
Meilichio a Pompei*, Naples 1991.

Essential plan of Pompeii, from
H. Eschebach-L. Eschebach,
*Pompeji vom 7. Jahrhundert v. Chr.
bis 79 n. Chr.*, Cologne-Weimar-
Vienna 1995

7, 37, 38: from *Pompei e gli
architetti francesi dell'Ottocento*,
Catalog of the exhibition
(Paris-Naples-Pompeii 1981),
Naples 1981, pp. 228,
fig. 78; p. 48, fig. 41; p. 69, fig. 43

3, 4, 5, 9, 10, 11, 13, 15, 16, 42,
53: from F. Mazois, *Les ruines de
Pompéi*, I-IV, Paris 1824-1838

6: from W. Gell, J. Gandy,
*Pompeiana. The Result of
Excavations since 1819*, I-II,
London 1832

12: from J.-P. Adam,
*La construction romaine. Matériaux
et techniques*, Picard, Paris 1984,
fig. 737

19, 31, 40: from J.-B. Piranèse,
*Antiquités de la Grande Grèce
aujourd'hui*, I, Paris 1837;
II, *Antiquités de Pompéi*, Paris 1837

1, 21, 43: from I.C. Richard Abbé
de Saint-Non, *Voyage pittoresque ou
Description du Royaume de Naples
et Sicile*, Paris 1781-1786
(reprinting supervised by R. Causa,
Naples 1981)

27: from A. Maiuri, "Studi e
ricerche sulle fortificazioni di
Pompei", *Monumenti Antichi
dell'Accademia dei Lincei* 33 (1930)

28: from E. La Rocca, M. and
A. de Vos, *Guida archeologica di
Pompei*, Milan 1981

33, 49, 50, 51: from
Soprintendenza Archeologica di
Napoli ADS, 916, 78, 79, 82

39, 44, 45: from Naples, Museo
Nazionale di San Martino,
inv. 13333, 13340, 13051

DISCOVERING POMPEII

Texts by
Antonio Varone [A.V.]
Fabrizio Pesando [F.P.]
Annamaria Ciarallo [A.C.]
Antonio d'Ambrosio [A.d'A.]
Lorenzo Fergola [L.F.]
Valeria Sampaolo [V.S.]

Photographs by
Fotografica Foglia s.a.s.

Illustrations by
Ludovico Bisi

Translation by
Federico Pool

Printed in 1998 on behalf
of Elemond Spa by Tipografica
La Piramide (Rome)